MEDICAL CONFIDENTIALITY
AND LEGAL PRIVILEGE

SOCIAL ETHICS AND POLICY SERIES
Edited by Anthony Dyson and John Harris
Centre for Social Ethics and Policy,
University of Manchester

EXPERIMENTS ON EMBRYOS
Anthony Dyson and John Harris (eds)

THE LIMITS OF MEDICAL PATERNALISM
Heta Häyry

PROTECTING THE VULNERABLE
Autonomy and Consent in Health Care
Margaret Brazier and Mary Lobjoit (eds)

MEDICAL
CONFIDENTIALITY
AND
LEGAL PRIVILEGE

Jean V. McHale

London and New York

First published 1993
by Routledge
11 New Fetter Lane, London EC4P 4EE

Simultaneously published in the USA and Canada
by Routledge
29 West 35th Street, New York, NY 10001

Reprinted 2002

Routledge is an imprint of the Taylor & Francis Group

© Jean V. McHale

Printed in Great Britain by
Hobbs The Printers Ltd, Totton, Hants

British Library Cataloguing in Publication Data
McHale, Jean V.
Medical Confidentiality and Legal Privilege. –
(Social Ethics & Policy Series)
I. Title II. Series
174

Library of Congress Cataloging in Publication Data
McHale, Jean V. (Jean Vanessa)
Medical confidentiality and legal privilege / Jean V. McHale.
p.   cm. – (Social ethics and policy series)
Includes bibliographical references and index.
1. Confidential communications–Physicians–Great Britain.
2. Medical records–Law and legislation–Great Britain. 3. AIDS
(Disease)–Law and legislation–Great Britain. I. Title. II. Series.
KD7519.P48M34   1993
344.41′0412–dc20
[344.104412]   92-26235
ISBN 0–415–04695–5

CONTENTS

PREFACE

This book would not have been written without the kindness and encouragement of a large number of people. I would like to thank particularly Professor Margaret Brazier, who encouraged me to write the book and whose endless patience and enthusiasm sustained me through the long writing process. Thanks are also due to Professor Martin Wasik who was my supervisor for my M.Phil. thesis which formed the basis for the book.

Several people have stoically waded through drafts of the book at various stages and made perceptive comments. I wish to thank Dr Mary Lobjoit, Professor A. O. Dyson, David Ormrod, Dr Marcus Ellis and Michael Gunn.

A number of medical practitioners also kindly gave up their time to talk to me about how medical confidentiality and the dilemmas of confidentiality in the courtroom appeared from the viewpoint of their own practice: Dr Mary Lobjoit, Dr Margaret Towse, Dr Marcus Ellis, Dr Michael Maresh and Dr Richard Burslem. I would also like to thank the editorial staff at Routledge for their kind assistance, in particular Virginia Myers and Pauline Marsh.

Last, but as the cliché says, by no means least, I wish to thank my parents and my friends, who have probably heard enough about medical confidentiality to last them several lifetimes!

TABLE OF CASES

1

SHOULD THE DOCTOR TELL?

Patients have traditionally expected doctors to keep their secrets and to maintain silence regarding their confidential information. If doctors break that obligation, they may be disciplined by their professional body, the General Medical Council, and find themselves defendants in an action in a court of law for breach of confidence. In the light of such an expectation many patients and doctors are surprised to be told that the doctor can be forced to give evidence in the courtroom about the patient's confidential information. That surprise borders on incredulity when they find that special rules of evidence protect lawyer–client information from disclosure. Why does this anomaly exist, and what is so important about confidential information anyway?

CRISIS IN CONFIDENTIALITY

The spread of AIDS has forced all those involved in health care to reassess the ethical obligations which they owe their patients and clients. How far should they allow respect for the autonomy of the individual patient to get in the way of the need for society to stop the spread of AIDS? Some of the most difficult dilemmas have arisen over the ethical obligation of confidentiality. A guarantee of confidentiality may be vital for the person who fears that he or she may have contracted HIV. Without that promise he (henceforth 'or she' is understood) may be unwilling to seek treatment and counselling, fearful of the repercussions to his home and family life should his HIV-positive status be disclosed.

However, while much of the recent controversy surrounding confidentiality as an ethical issue has been prompted by the AIDS crisis, concern relating to confidentiality in general is something which goes far deeper. It can be regarded as a consequence of a world in which the individual is finding it increasingly difficult to keep sensitive personal information from the scrutiny of others. Most major institutions hold large amounts of personal data. The Government holds records relating to tax and national insurance payments; banks and building societies hold information about our financial resources and about our commitments regarding, for example, our mortgage. Furthermore our employers have records relating to every aspect of our working lives from promotion to pensions. Concern has been expressed regarding the ease by which personal data can be transmitted between institutions and about the serious personal consequences ensuing if data are inaccurate or if unauthorised persons are able to gain access to those data. This danger has become more serious because of the increasing use of computers.

Responses have come from both Parliament and the courts. The equitable remedy of breach of confidence is increasingly used as a means of protecting personal confidential information from being disclosed to third parties without the consent of the person who imparted that information.[1] In addition, legislation has been enacted in an attempt to regulate data held on computer and in some manual files,[2] and the Computer Misuse Act 1990 was passed with the aim of tackling the problem of unauthorised access by computer hackers.

Medical information has traditionally been regarded as particularly confidential in nature.[3] It is not surprising, therefore, that the law has been used to protect medical confidences. So, for example, when the medical records of two general practitioners with AIDS were published in a national newspaper, the court were prepared to order that further publication should be restrained and made strong statements concerning the importance of keeping patient information and particularly AIDS patient information confidential.[4] Yet, despite this, if a doctor is called upon to give evidence in court about his patient's medical information, he must give evidence regardless of the wishes of his patient, or else he will be liable to be punished for being in contempt of court.[5] This lack of respect for medical confidences sits uneasily alongside protection given to other types of professional confidential information in the courtroom. This protection goes beyond lawyer–client confidences and extends to those, for example, who give information to the NSPCC regarding child abuse.[6] The confidentiality of police informers has been protected, and special provision also exists for journalists' sources.[7] Is English law in this area fundamentally inconsistent? Why is there such an emphasis on confidential information generally? How easy is it to justify legislation allowing patients to stop doctors testifying as they do in other jurisdictions? To begin to answer these questions we first need to consider just how confidential the doctor–patient relationship truly is.

CONFIDENTIAL: HOW CONFIDENTIAL?

Two dramatic dilemmas illustrate the problem. First, a married man of 43 goes to his GP. He has been suffering from persistent coughs and night sweats. He admits to being bi-sexual. His doctor, concerned about these symptoms, suggests tentatively that the man should take a test to determine whether he has contracted HIV. The patient agrees. When the patient next visits the doctor, the doctor gently breaks the news to him that he is indeed HIV positive and that he may go on to develop AIDS. When counselling the patient about the implications of this diagnosis the doctor asks whether he is still having sexual relations with his wife, and if so whether the patient is willing to tell her of the diagnosis. The patient refuses. The doctor explains the risks to the patient's wife, but still the patient refuses because he is scared of the effect that the revelation could have on his marriage. He tells the doctor that his wife has never known that he is bi-sexual. The doctor is faced with a terrible dilemma. Should he go ahead and break confidence? If he fails to do so the wife may contract the virus, though the risk may be less if the couple engage in safe sex practices. Yet, if he does breach that confidence he will probably have fractured irretrievably his relationship with his patient at a time when medical care and the patient's trust in his doctor are vital. His ethical code, promulgated by the General Medical Council, provides an exception to the general duty of confidentiality when this is in the public interest. Should this doctor tell?

Second, a medical practitioner is telephoned by a senior partner in a firm of solicitors. The conversation proceeds as follows: 'A client of mine is a patient held under a restriction order in a psychiatric hospital. The medical report from his hospital psychiatrist is encouraging, and we have decided to go ahead with an application to a Mental Health Review Tribunal for him to be discharged. Would you please examine him and give us your opinion?' The psychiatrist agrees. He meets the patient, examines him, and duly compiles the report. Far from finding the patient is suitable for discharge, the report says that he is a particularly dangerous individual with a personality that is probably of a psychopathic deviant nature. When the report is sent to the solicitors, they decide to withdraw the case from the tribunal. The doctor, however, wants the hospital and the Home Office to know the contents of the report, as he believes that it is information which should be taken into account in deciding if a future transfer should take place. Should the doctor send a copy of the report to the hospital and the Home Office against the express wishes of the patient and his solicitors?

Would either or both of these medical practitioners be right to breach confidence? In the first example, if the GP tells the patient's wife, this would probably mean that the danger to her would be reduced. But this could be at the cost of the patient's relationship with his GP. At the same time a cloak of confidentiality may be imperative for such a patient. The consequences of its becoming publicly known that a person is HIV positive can be devastating, including social ostracism, rejection by family or friends and isolation at a time when the support of others is vital. Other patients who suspect that they too may have contracted HIV may not come forward for tests, fearful that their confidentiality could be at risk. But should the medical practitioner leave the wife in danger? If he does tell her of her husband's condition, she might not act adversely but might provide a valuable source of support and encouragement.

The dilemma of whether or not to break confidence in the case of the psychiatric patient is equally problematic. The doctor, by divulging the report, could ensure that a potentially highly dangerous person was not released into the community, but what is his obligation to his patient? Should he disclose when he thinks that a patient is clearly psychopathic, or liable to be dangerous? What level of danger should exist before he discloses? Or is there no normal obligation of confidence at all in a situation in which a medical practitioner sees a patient to conduct a psychiatric examination for one specific purpose and may never see him again?

These are extreme examples. Confidentiality in everyday practice presents less dramatic situations; but even here there are difficult issues regarding the scope of confidentiality to be resolved. How realistic is it to talk about confidentiality in the context of a modern community practice or in a hospital where information may be passed on freely from one staff member to another during the care of the patient? The fact that an ethical obligation may be uncertain is not a reason why it should be summarily abandoned. The fact that in some situations the doctor may feel constrained to breach confidence after making a difficult moral judgment does not mean that the ethic of confidentiality is worthless.

It is important, though, to illustrate some of these problems at an early stage. If patients should be able to stop their doctor from testifying in the courtroom on the grounds of the inherently confidential nature of medical information, it will be of great help to determine exactly which medical information is 'confidential' and which is not. These issues will be returned to later. In the rest of this chapter, I consider why it is that a patient may seek a remedy in order to stop a doctor breaking confidence by selling the story of his treatment to a national newspaper, but at the same time, the law of breach of confidence is impotent as a means of helping a patient who wants to stop disclosure of his medical records in the courtroom.

RESTRAINING DISCLOSURE OF CONFIDENTIAL INFORMATION

The law has long been used as a means of protecting confidential medical information. In the eighteenth century, in the case of *Wood v Wyatt*, publication of the diaries of the doctor of George III was restrained.[8] But protection of the confidential medical information of lesser mortals came somewhat later. The remedy of breach of confidence is a means by which those who have entrusted confidential information to others may restrain disclosure of that information which takes place without their consent. It is an area of law which has expanded considerably in recent years. The litigant who wants to stop disclosure may ask the court for an injunction to prohibit such disclosure. Where disclosure has already occurred, he will seek damages in compensation for that disclosure. The action for breach of confidence has been described by the Law Commission as being

> a civil remedy affording protection against the disclosure or use of information which is not publicly known and which has been entrusted to a person in circumstances imposing an obligation not to disclose or use that information without the authority of the person who imparted it.[9]

Although much of the early case-law was concerned with its use to restrain unauthorised disclosure of commercial information and trade secrets, increasingly the remedy has been used as a means of safeguarding information of an inherently personal and private nature. In *Argyll v Argyll* (1967) it was held that communications between husband and wife were pursuant to 'the normal confidence and trust between husband and wife' and thus publication in a national newspaper was restrained.[10]

Similarly, in the more recent case of *Stephens v Avery* (1988) it was held that information concerning a lesbian affair communicated in confidence by the plaintiff to the defendant, her close friend, who then divulged the details to a tabloid newspaper, would be protected by the courts.[11]

The courts have been particularly anxious to prevent confidences between doctor and patient from being divulged. In the case of *X v Y* (1988) two general practitioners were diagnosed as having contracted HIV.[12] They underwent treatment at a local hospital. The treatment took the form of counselling intended to help the patient to come to terms with the fact that he is HIV positive and to suggest precautions to avoid transmitting the condition to others. The GPs decided to continue with their medical practice. An employee of the health authority passed the medical records of these doctors to a journalist, who used them as the basis for an article in a tabloid newspaper. The health authority sought an injunction to prevent publication. At trial it was asserted that the records had been disclosed in breach of a duty of confidence. The defendants argued that while they had received the relevant information in breach of confidence, they were still right to go ahead and publish the story. The fact that there were two practising GPs who were HIV positive, they argued, was information that was clearly in the public interest. They relied upon *dicta* in earlier case-law to back up their arguments. In *Fraser v Evans* (1969)[13] Lord Denning had said that 'there are some things which may be required to be disclosed in the public interest in which event no confidence can be prayed in aid to keep them secret',[14] and similarly Stephenson LJ had said in *Lion Laboratories v Evans* (1984)[15] that

> there is confidential information which the public may have a right to receive and others, in particular the press may have a right or even a duty to publish even if the information has been obtained in flagrant breach of confidence and irrespective of the motive of the informer.[16]

In *X v Y* the newspaper argued that there were two main reasons why publication of the names of the HIV-positive doctors was in the public interest. First, the court should protect the freedom of the press and assert the importance of the value of free speech, especially with regard to the media. Second, the public's attention needed to be drawn to the dangers of the AIDS virus being passed on by a practising doctor, for example during the course of a medical examination. In addition the public should be aware of the fact that since one of the results of developing AIDS is that the patient may gradually develop dementia, an individual's judgment could be impaired without this being obvious to a casual observer. A GP could continue to treat patients in a situation in which his judgment was impaired, which could have potentially very serious and even tragic consequences.

In contrast, as the plaintiff, the health authority regarded the public interest as falling squarely upon the side of preserving confidentiality for patients generally, and for AIDS sufferers in particular special safeguards were used to protect the anonymity of sufferers. For example they are referred to in medical records by false names. But this anonymity was under threat. It was claimed that press representatives had attempted to gain entry to the hospital posing as relatives or on the pretext of bringing flowers. A staff nurse had been offered money if she would provide information about a patient.

Rose J granted the injunction. Though acknowledging that there were strong interests both in press freedom and in knowing what the defendants wanted to publish, he stressed that

> The records of hospital patients, particularly those suffering from this appalling condition, should in my judgment be as confidential as the courts can possibly make them in order that the plaintiffs may be free from suspicion that they are harbouring disloyal employees.[17]

He was also influenced in his conclusions by the fact that a wide-ranging debate concerning the effect of AIDS upon sufferers in general and upon members of the medical profession in particular was already taking place.

The judgment clearly shows that there is judicial recognition of the importance of safeguarding medical confidentiality, particularly when the patient is suffering from an illness which, by its very nature, necessitates complete confidentiality for the patient. An AIDS sufferer who has had his identity disclosed may suffer social ostracism and abuse. However, this legal obligation of confidence is not absolute and it can be overridden where that is in the public interest. In *X v Y* the judge simply found the defendants' public-interest argument unconvincing.

Successful invocation of the public-interest defence to justify the disclosure of confidential medical information can be seen in the subsequent case of *W v Egdell* (1989).[18] W was detained in a secure hospital under a restriction order after a plea of diminished responsibility to his charge of murder had been accepted. Some eight years after he was sentenced his medical officer at the hospital considered that W's medical condition was such that he could be transferred from the hospital to a regional secure unit (this is a half-way house between a secure hospital and discharge from an institution). This recommendation was rejected by the Home Office. W then decided, on the strength of the favourable reports he had received from the hospital, to apply to a Mental Health Review Tribunal to be discharged from hospital altogether. Dr Egdell was instructed by W's solicitors to carry out an examination of W and to prepare a report to support W's application to the tribunal. On receiving Dr Egdell's report, which was highly unfavourable to W, W's solicitors decided to withdraw the application to the tribunal. Dr Egdell, on finding that the report had not been sent to the hospital, took it upon himself to send a copy to the hospital director. He further agreed that a copy be sent to the Home Office. By this time the Home Secretary had already referred the case to the tribunal as he was bound to do, because the case had not been before the tribunal within the preceding three years. The plaintiffs tried to restrain the defendants from using the report. They argued that there was a doctor–patient relationship between W and Dr Egdell and that he was therefore bound by the obligation of confidentiality.

At first instance Scott J rejected the claim that disclosure should be restrained. In his opinion the doctor owed a duty not only to W but also to the public. This required him to place before the proper authorities the results of his examination of W. He stressed that W was not an ordinary member of the public. He placed weight upon the fact that, while in detention, W had been seen by a number of psychiatrists. All of these owed him a duty of confidence such that they could not, for example, sell the information to a newspaper, but at the same time the reports compiled about W were on file and were available to the Home Office. In the view of Scott J, the fact that these reports were on file had not inhibited W in his dealings with those psychiatrists, so why should Dr Egdell be treated any differently?

W appealed to the Court of Appeal. Though all three judges in the Court of Appeal rejected the appeal, it is interesting to contrast the approach taken by the two judges who delivered full judgments. Sir Stephen Brown, the President, was broadly in agreement with the first-instance decision. Disclosure of the information was in the public interest in ensuring the safety of the public as a whole. The effect of suppressing the material contained in the report would have been to deprive both the hospital and the Secretary of State of vital information. In his judgment, the other judge, Lord Justice Bingham, was far more concerned to emphasise the importance of preserving confidentiality in the case of a patient such as W. A patient held under a restriction order must be able to have recourse to a professional advisor who is independent and discreet. Such a patient should only have the confidentiality of his personal information limited where this was justified on the grounds of the exception contained in the medical profession's ethical codes on the grounds of the doctor's duty to society. On the facts of the particular case, however, his Lordship held that the disclosure was indeed justified. The decisive facts were that

> Where a man has committed multiple killings under the disability of serious mental illness decisions which may lead directly or indirectly to his release from hospital should not be made unless a responsible authority is able to make an informed judgment that the risk of repetition is so small as to be acceptable.[19]

Both the judgment at first instance and those of the Court of Appeal illustrate that confidentiality is a far from absolute obligation in the eyes of the courts. It is simply one factor of the public interest which needs to be weighed against other relevant factors of public interest, such as the need to ensure that the public at large are not placed at risk of serious harm by the untoward release of a particular individual. But even in the present example the fact that Dr Egdell was acting in the public interest to disclose the information regarding W to the hospital did not mean that he would have been acting in the public interest had he decided to ring one of the leading tabloid newspapers and give them his story to be printed under the heading 'Why psychopathic killer shouldn't be released'.

The case of *W v Egdell* is not, I suggest, an indication that the courts are resiling from the protection of medical confidentiality as such. What it does illustrate is that the protection given is by no means absolute. The approach taken by the courts in many ways reflects that taken by medical practice. The judges referred to the fact that the medical profession themselves sanction breaches of confidentiality in their ethical code and that one of the exceptions expressly provided for in the General Medical Council's professional code of ethics is that disclosure may be justifiable if it is in the public interest.

W v Egdell was followed in the later case of *R v Crozier* (1990),[20] where the Court of Appeal again expressed their opinion that disclosure of medical information by an examining psychiatrist is in the public interest. Crozier had been detained in a hospital under a restriction order. The facts concerned his detention, which came after his trial for the attempted murder of his sister-in-law. Dr M was instructed to examine Crozier and make a report for the defence. The report did not arrive in time for the hearing. On the day of the hearing Dr M arrived in court just as the judge was passing sentence. He approached counsel for the Crown and said that Crozier was suffering from a mental illness of a psychopathic nature and should be detained in a maximum security unit. The Crown appealed and obtained variation of sentence. The defendant lodged an appeal arguing that Dr M had given his report to the Crown in breach of his duty of confidentiality owed to Crozier as his patient.

Lord Justice Watkins held that Dr M was right in making the disclosure and that it was clearly in the public interest for information about such a dangerous patient to be disclosed. Disclosure was particularly justified here in view of the fact that Dr M also knew that the original psychiatrist Dr W, who had seen Crozier at first and had at that time pronounced him sane, had changed his mind.

Although the protection provided is not absolute, the impact that the law of breach of confidence might have upon the doctor–patient relationship must not be underestimated. As the judgment in *X v Y* showed, the courts will be vigilant to safeguard confidential information in appropriate circumstances. Given the fact that it is an effective remedy outside the courtroom, could it ever be used as a means by which a patient might restrain a breach of confidence where his doctor was called to give evidence in court against the wishes of his patient?

Academics have argued for some time over whether an injunction would issue in such a situation.[21] It appears from recent dicta, however, that the courts are unlikely to use the equitable remedy of the injunction as a means of expanding the law of evidential privilege. In the case of *Goddard v Nationwide Building Society* (1987),[22] Nourse LJ stated firmly that: 'It cannot be the function of equity to accord a *de facto* privilege to communications in respect of which no privilege can be claimed "Equity follows the law".'[23] Such an extension of the law of equity would in any case, it is submitted, be undesirable.

Doctor–patient relationships are not uniformly confidential, as illustrated earlier. A closer look needs to be given to the nature of the doctor–patient relationship to pinpoint those areas which are confidential and those which are not. This is not a task which should be left to a court to determine on each occasion on which a patient decides that he does not want his medical records produced. For a patient in such a situation to have to bring a separate action seeking an injunction would also at the very least be highly wasteful of resources. If such a reform is needed, and if the confidential nature of the doctor–patient relationship warrants protection, then some thought should also be given to the impact which such protection might have on different areas of litigation, and some broad policy decisions may be required. *Ad hoc* judicial development, it is submitted, is not an adequate substitute for such an enquiry.

This book discusses how English law has come to reject any special recognition for the doctor–patient privilege in law and asks the question: Should the doctor tell? I look at two possible justifications for a privilege which have been advanced in other jurisdictions to see if either or both are strong enough as a basis for an English privilege statute. They are utilitarianism and a human rights-based justification. The complex nature of modern-day medical practice is then considered, and I ask the reader to consider if medical confidentiality is reality or rhetoric. Practical issues which need to be tackled should any reform be attempted are then discussed. If a privilege should be enacted, what form should it take? For example should it apply in all areas of litigation or, as in many states in America, should its application be limited to civil cases only? Who should be classified as a doctor for the purposes of the privilege? Should the alternative medical practitioner be included alongside your GP? What about psychotherapists and nurse practitioners? The impact of such a statute is discussed in a concluding chapter with reference to the many areas of litigation in which it is likely that such a statute would be raised by the patient.

2

COMPARISONS AND INCONSISTENCIES

The patient can stop his doctor from disclosing details of his confidential information in virtually all situations save in the court-room. The courts have refused to recognise any special rule of evidence which would give the patient that right. But why have they consistently rejected such a privilege? Why is it that while certain professional confidential information is protected, other professional information is not? If lawyer–client confidences are protected, then why not doctor–patient? Why protect the confidentiality of journalists' sources and of other sources of information given in confidence, for example to the NSPCC, and yet exclude medical confidential information? Does this represent a fundamental inconsistency in the protection of personal information at trial? If it does, then it should be remedied. Or is the answer that information is safeguarded not because of the fact that it is confidential *per se* but on other grounds? If this is the case, then perhaps the time has come for some reconsideration of the protection of confidential information in the courtroom.

REJECTION OF A DOCTOR–PATIENT PRIVILEGE IN ENGLISH LAW

The patient will find absolutely no support for a claim of doctor–patient privilege in decided cases relating to evidential privilege, and this steadfast opposition has been mirrored in the writings of academics and English law-reform bodies. But what exactly is 'evidential privilege'? According to Cross, 'A witness is said to be privileged when he may validly claim not to answer a question or to supply information which would be relevant to the determination of an issue in judicial proceedings'.[1]

Privilege is thus a means by which evidence is excluded from the scrutiny of the court or other tribunal of fact. It matters not whether that evidence is of relatively little importance to the ultimate resolution of the case or whether it is of crucial importance.

From as far back as the *Duchess of Kingston's Case* in 1776 the courts have refused to recognise a physician–patient privilege.[2] That case was a trial for bigamy. Mr Hawkins, a physician who had attended the accused and her alleged husband, was asked: 'Do you know from the parties of any marriage between them?' He replied: 'I do not know how far anything which has come before me in a confidential trust in my profession should be disclosed consistent with my professional honour.' Lord Chief Justice Mansfield in response said:

> If all your Lordships will acquiesce, Mr Hawkins will understand that it is your judgment and opinion that a surgeon has no privilege where it is a material question in a civil or a criminal cause to know whether the parties were married or whether a child was born, to say that this introduction to the parties was in the course of his profession and that in that way he came to knowledge of it. If a surgeon was voluntarily to reveal these secrets, to be sure he would be guilty of a breach of honour and a grave indiscretion, but to give that information in a court of justice which by the law of the land he is bound to do will never be imputed to him as an indiscretion whatever.

The mere fact that information had been given in confidence and that the recipient of that information had bound himself not to disclose that information to third parties did not mean that it should be removed from the scrutiny of the court. In *Wheelar v Le Marchant*[3] in 1881, Jessel MR further repudiated any suggestion of a doctor–patient privilege:

> the principle protecting confidential information is of a very limited character ... The communications made to a medical man by his patient as to the probable origins of the disease from which he is suffering and which must necessarily be made in order to enable the medical man to advise or prescribe are not protected.[4]

In *Garner v Garner* (1920)[5] the court confirmed that disclosure could be ordered even in relation to information concerning venereal disease which was required to be kept confidential by statute. Mrs

Garner was petitioning for divorce on the grounds of adultery and cruelty. She claimed that her husband had transmitted syphilis to her and wanted her husband's medical records to support her claim. Objection was made to production of the medical records on the grounds that the hospital had adopted the National Scheme in relation to the treatment of venereal disease. The statutory regulations under which the scheme was operated required absolute secrecy. Despite the fact that secrecy was important for the operation of the scheme, McCardie J ordered the medical information to be disclosed in the interests of justice. The approach taken in these early cases is reflected in more recent judgments. In *Nuttall v Nuttall and Twynan* (1964),[6] the husband in a divorce suit hearing subpoenaed as a witness a psychiatrist who had been consulted by the wife and co-respondent. When called to testify the psychiatrist said that the information was protected by professional confidentiality. Edgedale J said that what a person said to a doctor in a professional consultation was not privileged, and the witness must either give evidence or be committed to prison for contempt of court. A similar approach was taken in *Hunter v Mann* (1974).[7] That case involved a car accident. Both driver and passenger left the scene of the accident and could not be traced. The car which they had been driving had been taken without the consent of its owner. On the same day as the accident a doctor treated a man in his evening surgery and later that evening at the man's request he treated a girl who said that she had been involved in a car accident. The doctor told both the man and the girl to report the incident to the police, but they failed to do so. Subsequently the police asked the doctor to reveal the identities of the two patients, relying upon section 168 (3) of the Road Traffic Act 1972. This provided that

> Where the driver of a vehicle is alleged to be guilty of an offence to which this subsection applies . . . (b) any other person shall if required as aforesaid give any information which is in his power to give and which may lead to the identification of the driver.

The doctor claimed that this was confidential information which he should not be required to disclose. Boreham J held that the doctor had no right to refuse to disclose confidential information during the course of judicial proceedings. The other member of the court, Lord Widgery, did, however, suggest that there were certain circumstances in which the judge, exercising his discretion, could refuse to compel the doctor to testify concerning confidential information: 'The judge by virtue of the overriding discretion to control his court which all

English judges have, can, if he thinks fit, tell the doctor that he need not answer the question.[8] A judicial discretion is something very different from an evidential privilege. A privilege means that the evidence will be automatically excluded at the hearing unless there is some recognised rule justifying disclosure. A discretion, in contrast, is a balancing test in which the judiciary weigh up various policy considerations before deciding whether evidence should be excluded. (This must not be confused with the public-policy exclusionary rule, which will be dealt with shortly.) It may be argued that if the judiciary were prepared to make use of their discretionary power, then there would be no need for any special privilege. Lord Widgery's suggestion is considered later in this chapter.

From the above cases it is clear that there is no general rule of privilege which will enable a patient to stop admission of his medical information. The refusal of the judiciary to extend the categories of evidential privilege to cover that of doctor and patient has been accompanied by the unwillingness of law-reform bodies to support proposals for such a privilege.

The Criminal Law Revision Committee considered the question in their Eleventh Report.[9] Evidence was submitted to the Committee that the privilege was necessary in the public interest to ensure that individuals seek medical advice where necessary, and that people should feel free to talk to their doctor about something, even if it is embarrassing or discreditable, without the fear that the doctor may have to give evidence of it in court. The Committee held that while there might be grounds for saying that psychiatrist–patient information should be privileged, enacting such a privilege would lead to insuperable difficulties. This was because an overlap existed between psychiatric medicine and other areas of medical practice. It could mean that the general doctor–patient relationship could be protected as well as the psychiatrist–patient relationship. But if patients suffering from mental illness are in need of such protection, then why should that protection be denied simply because on occasion they may receive treatment from practitioners other than specialists in psychiatry/psychotherapy? Psychiatric illness is one of the most confidential areas of medical practice. Why not grant a privilege to all patients receiving treatment for sensitive ailments of that type generally? The Criminal Law Revision Committee seem to have been influenced by the thought that too much evidence might be excluded from the courtroom. But there is a danger in overestimating the level of exclusion which could result. Several other nations in which such

15

privileges have been introduced have succeeded in applying them without any major disruption to the legal process.[10]

INCONSISTENCY OF APPROACH

Confidentiality then, is, no protective cloak to the litigant who wants to safeguard his medical information. But, despite this rejection of confidentiality as a basis of an exclusionary rule of evidence, the courts do already protect information which is 'confidential' in nature from being disclosed in court. The confidences which pass between client and lawyer for the purposes of litigation are protected from disclosure by legal professional privilege. Moreover, in a number of cases, public policy intervenes to prevent disclosure of information which is confidential in nature, on the grounds of the public interest. For example the identity of those persons supplying information to the NSPCC concerning children who have been subject to abuse has been protected from disclosure.[11] Journalists are able to restrain disclosure of their sources of information in certain situations.[12] Surely the courts are being inconsistent in rejecting confidentiality as a basis for the doctor–patient privilege while at the same time they uphold the confidentiality of this type of information?

But, despite this apparent inconsistency, on closer examination we find that the courts are not protecting the inherent confidentiality of information as such: rather the information is protected because of various other, separate public-policy considerations.

THE LITIGATION PRIVILEGE

Legal professional privilege shields from disclosure communications which take place between legal advisor and client and between legal advisor and third parties when these are for the purposes of litigation.[13] At first glance there appear to be several similarities between the lawyer–client relationship and the doctor–patient relationship. Both are professional relationships. Both give rise to a need to ensure that client/patient confidences are respected. Though frequently the actual nature of the communications differs between the relationships – the lawyer–client relationship may involve the exchange of confidential information concerning a broken commercial contract, for example – on occasion they may be of a similar sensitive personal nature. Examples of this are the client discussing with his lawyer the breakdown of his marriage or the nature and extent of injuries which he has received in an accident. On closer examination, however, the apparent inconsistency between allowing lawyer–client privilege and denying doctor–patient privilege is shown to be illusory. It is clear that the lawyer–client relationship is given especial protection in the law of evidence, not because of its inherent confidentiality, but rather because of considerations of the smooth administration of justice.

The rationale behind legal professional privilege was examined by Jessel MR in the case of *Anderson v Bank of British Columbia* (1886).[14] The rule was necessary so that the client 'should be able to make a clean breast of it to the gentleman whom he consults with a view to the prosecution of his claim or the substantiating his defence against the claim of others'.[15] The reason for the protection of lawyer–client relationships in this way is tied to the notion of the English trial being an inherently adversarial process. Both parties would find that it was impossible to conduct their case effectively without a privilege. The discussions of the lawyer with his client, with witnesses and other related parties could automatically be used as evidence. In criminal cases there would be a very grave danger that lawyers would in effect become one of the arms of the criminal investigation process. The lawyer would have to make it clear to his clients that whatever they said might be taken down and used in evidence against them!

There have, however, been some cases in which the courts have given indications that the privilege protection is attached to the lawyer–client relationship by virtue of the fact that it is a confidential professional relationship and not because of the way in which it facilitates litigation. So, in *Greenough v Gaskell* (1833)[16] the view was advanced that *all* lawyer–client communications were privileged. In *Minter v Priest* (1930)[17] Lord Buckmaster held that, while not all communications would be held to be privileged, a generous interpretation would be given to what came within the privilege. But in other cases a more limited approach has been taken and in the more recent case of *Balabel v Air India* (1988),[18] while he stressed that the boundaries of the privilege were not static, Taylor LJ said that the *dicta* in earlier cases indicating a broad approach to lawyer–client privilege were too wide and that a far more restricted approach should be taken to limit the scope of the privilege within justifiable bounds. This reflects the fact that this privilege is removing from the scrutiny of the court often highly relevant information, and any such exclusion needs to be justified. The role of the solicitor has expanded, and the expansion seems set to continue. If all communications between a client and his solicitor were to be privileged, that could unduly hamper the fact-finding process. The courts appear to be striking a balance between the need to facilitate the administration of justice by ensuring that individuals can get legal advice unhampered by the fear that what they say could be used against them, and the need to ensure that the privilege is not so wide as to remove unjustifiably relevant evidence from the courts' scrutiny.

The fact that the privilege exists primarily to further considerations of the administration of justice and not simply to protect professional confidences is illustrated by decided cases. While privilege has been held to cover communications between a solicitor and third parties where these are for the purposes of litigation, the courts have stressed that these communications will be privileged only if the dominant purpose for their occurrence was that litigation was pending. So, for example, in *Waugh v British Railways Board* (1980),[19] the plaintiff's husband, who was an employee of the defendant, was killed in a railway accident. The plaintiff asked for discovery of an internal report which the defendants had compiled relating to the accident. It was held in the House of Lords that while one of the reasons why the report had been compiled was related to the forthcoming litigation, it was not the dominant purpose behind the preparation of the report. The claim was rejected. Similarly it has recently been held that where information comes into solicitors' hands during litigation which would not otherwise be privileged, the simple fact that this information is handled by solicitors does not by itself serve to impose privilege protection.[20]

It must be emphasised that this lawyer–client privilege is not absolute in nature. The policy of ensuring that litigation is facilitated gives way on occasion to other interests related to the administration of justice. Communications between legal advisor and client where these are for the purpose of litigation may not be privileged if the evidence is necessary to establish the innocence of a defendant.[21] In that situation the public interest in the smooth running of the adversarial system is outweighed by the interests of justice. Second, the privilege will not apply if the purpose of the consultation was to enable the client to commit a crime or to perpetrate a fraud. This has been justified according to Stephen J in *R v Cox and Railton* (1884)[22] on the grounds that otherwise a man who intended to commit treason or murder could take legal advice for the purposes of doing so with impunity.

So even if there is, in fact, sufficient justification for protecting

18

doctor–patient confidentiality in the courtroom just as we protect lawyer–client confidentiality, we are still left with the problem that strong countervailing public interests, such as the need to prevent a defendant from being disadvantaged in a criminal trial through relevant evidence being excluded, will need to be considered.

PUBLIC-POLICY EXCLUSIONS

In addition to the lawyer–client privilege the court will exclude confidential personal information if its exclusion satisfies considerations of public policy. Originally this rule was confined simply to issues of vital importance to the State. For example in the leading case of *Duncan v Cammell Laird* (1942),[23] an action was brought claiming damages for loss suffered as a result of the negligent construction of a submarine, the *Thetis*. The submarine had sunk and all her crew had perished. Relatives of the deceased sought disclosure of documents relating to the construction of the submarine. The defendants were instructed by the Admiralty to object to discovery in their capacity as Government contractors. The House of Lords refused disclosure. The interests of the State would be threatened by the disclosure of important military information such as that concerning the structure of the submarine, particularly in wartime.

Traditionally the courts have used public-policy grounds to justify the exclusion of evidence relating to police sources of information because of the need to facilitate the investigation of crime. This was extended to cover information supplied by the police to the Gaming Board, an agency which issues gaming licences.[24] The Board obtains information from various sources, including the police, regarding applications for these licences. One Rogers had his application for a licence from the Board rejected and decided to bring an action against the police. To enable him to do this he sought disclosure of information supplied by the police to the Gaming Board. The House of Lords rejected his claim on the grounds that to allow disclosure could damage the workings of an important public service. The simple fact that this information was 'confidential' was not the decisive factor. The considerations of importance related to the public nature of the role of the Gaming Board and the practical issue that if information relating to the sources were made public, there would very probably be grave problems in getting information about the background of persons who had applied for licences.

The extent to which the public-policy rule could apply to protect information purely and simply because the information was 'confidential' in nature was one which was addressed by the House of Lords in an important later case, that of *D v National Society for the Prevention of Cruelty to Children* (NSPCC) (1978).[25] The NSPCC is a charity concerned with the welfare of children. It investigates complaints that children have been maltreated. It was also given the power under section 18 (1) of the Children and Young Persons Act 1969 to bring care proceedings. An allegation had been made to the Society that a child was being maltreated. The Society sent one of its inspectors to investigate the complaint. The allegations were found to be false: the child had been well treated. The health of the child's mother had been affected by the allegations, and she issued a writ against the NSPCC claiming damages for failure to exercise reasonable care to investigate the complaint. She also applied for an order that the Society should disclose to her all the documents in its possession relating to the identity of the person who made the false allegations against her. The Society opposed disclosure, arguing that it was extremely important that the confidentiality of its sources was preserved. Without guaranteed confidentiality individuals might well be discouraged from coming forward to give information. The House of Lords rejected the application for disclosure.

This decision is important for two reasons. First, if on examination of the speeches we discover that the evidence was excluded primarily because of its inherently confidential nature, this would appear to be inconsistent with the clear rejection in case-law of the doctor–patient privilege. Second, if a public-policy rule is used to exclude information of one type, could it not be used to protect confidential information of another type?

In the Court of Appeal Lord Denning placed very great weight upon the value of confidentiality

> when information has been imparted in confidence and particularly where there is a pledge to keep it confidential the courts should respect that confidentiality. They should in no way compel a breach of it save where the public interest clearly demands it and then only to the extent to which the public interest so requires.[26]

While conceding that there was no separate evidential privilege, Lord Denning, using his innovative skill, suggested the use of a presumption against disclosure unless that disclosure was in the public interest. His approach was not followed in the House of Lords.

Their Lordships robustly rejected the notion that there was any public interest in safeguarding confidentiality itself in the law of evidence. But confidential information may be protected if there is a sufficiently strong public interest in doing so. Lord Hailsham held that the welfare of children, particularly those at risk of harm, had been a concern of the Crown from early history.[27] It was an important consideration in this particular case that the NSPCC was one of only three classes of authorities which could bring care proceedings under the Children and Young Persons Act 1969. There was a public interest, he said, that the party able to bring care proceedings should receive information under a cloak of confidentiality. Whether it was the police or the local authority or the NSPCC, they were all entitled to claim protection for the confidentiality of their sources. As Lord Diplock said:

> The private promise of confidentiality must yield to the general public interest that in the administration of justice truth will out unless by reason of the character of the information or the relationship of the recipient of the information to the informant a more important public interest is served by protecting the information or the identity of the informant in a court of law.[28]

It seems clear, then, that there is no inconsistency between the refusal to grant a doctor–patient evidential privilege and the existence in the law of evidence of a public-policy exclusionary rule which has the effect of excluding certain information of an inherently confidential character. The mere fact that information is confidential is no automatic justification for privilege protection. If, however, we were able to show a sufficiently strong public-policy interest for excluding doctor–patient confidences, then would the courts be willing to extend the public-policy exclusionary rule to protect that type of information? In *D v NSPCC* Lord Hailsham stated that the categories of public interest are never closed and must alter from time to time whether by restriction or extension as social conditions and social legislation develop.[29] Surely there is a weighty public-policy interest in ensuring that patient medical information is kept confidential? Confidentiality is needed to ensure that patients come forward for treatment if they have contracted, or if they fear they have contracted, HIV or AIDS. This was emphasised by Rose J in *X v Y* (1988):[30]

21

The records of hospital patients, particularly those suffering from this appalling condition, should, in my judgment, be as confidential as the courts can properly make them in order that the plaintiffs may be free from suspicion that they are harbouring disloyal employees.[31]

Does the danger that the spread of HIV poses to our society and the high profile that the confidentiality of medical information has been given mean that the public-interest exclusionary rule should be expanded to accommodate treatment and counselling for HIV? And what about other types of medical treatment which depend heavily on a guarantee of confidentiality? Take psychiatric care, for example. Psychiatric treatment, as we shall see in chapter 4, is one of the most sensitive areas of medical practice. Many people regard those who suffer from any form of mental condition as in some way stigmatised. It is surely in the public interest that persons should feel free to come forward for treatment and therapy. Should the public-interest exclusionary rule be modified to take account of this interest? Since Lord Hailsham's comments in *D v NSPCC* that the categories of public interest are not closed there has been no mass expansion of the category of public interest, although in specific cases the claim that information should be kept confidential in the public interest has been upheld. The public-interest rule has been used to shield access to confidential information collected by organisations and Government departments.[32]

There has, however, been one recent case in which the courts have indicated that they might be moving in the direction of recognising exclusion of medical evidence on public-interest grounds. In *Re C* (1991),[33] the most recent civil-law case on the question of excluding medical information, the court suggested that the admission of medical evidence was something which was a matter for the use of judicial discretion. A mother agreed to have her child adopted. Later, however, she decided to withdraw her consent. It was alleged that the consent had been unreasonably withheld. A doctor's report on the mother's state of health was sought. The mother argued that admission of the evidence should not be allowed since it would amount to a breach of duty between doctor and patient.

The Court of Appeal, while deciding that the decision of the judge of first instance allowing the evidence to be admitted should be upheld, viewed the issue as a matter for the court's discretion. The court came to the conclusion that the adoption of a child was a very serious matter and therefore it was extremely important that all relevant evidence should be before the court. While two members of the Court of Appeal, Sir Stephen Brown and Stuart Smith LJ, talked generally in terms of judicial discretion to exclude evidence, the third member, Mann LJ, considered the admission of evidence from a public-interest viewpoint. His Lordship held:

> Let it be assumed, and I do not decide that such issue is before the court. If it be the law, the judge who is asked to admit the evidence of the doctor in relation to the treatment of his patient has to perform a balancing exercise. However, before undertaking the balance, he must consider whether the evidence which is proposed to be tendered would involve a breach of duty of confidence which it is in the public interest to preserve.

He went on to say that there was a strong public interest in the future life of a child and that here admission of the evidence was correct.

Mann LJ's judgment is, however, the sole pronouncement on this question. There is no indication that the courts have moved in the Denning direction of providing that confidentiality is presumed unless there is proof otherwise. It is perhaps questionable whether the most satisfactory solution to the problem is to let the courts evolve the public-policy rule over time and hope that perhaps one day an enlightened judiciary may extend it to protect medical confidentiality.[34] Even if the other judges were willing to follow Mann LJ's lead, it is doubtful if the public-policy exclusionary rule is the best method of excluding medical information. It lacks the precise definition that a specific statutory defined privilege may provide. Any privilege should, I suggest, contain a considered response to the problem posed by the variable levels of confidentiality which exist in medical practice.

Thus, on closer examination, the apparent inconsistency in the level of protection given to various types of confidential information is seen to be illusory. Those professional confidences which are protected at present in English law are given such protection because of other factors than their inherent confidentiality as such. In *D v NSPCC* the House of Lords were heavily influenced in their decision by the fact that the NSPCC was one of only a limited number of public agencies which can bring care proceedings. In *Rogers v Secretary of State for the Home Department* the Gaming Board had a public duty to issue gaming licences. As far as legal professional privilege is concerned, the lawyer's duty to his client is regarded as particularly important because without it the adversarial process would become unworkable. All these cases are decided on the basis that the smooth running of the legal system and its agencies must be protected. Where information ceased to be for the purpose of litigation, courts would be unwilling to grant privilege.[35]

The rejection of the doctor–patient privilege has been accompanied by the rejection of privilege in the case of another relationship often seen as inherently confidential, that of priest and penitent.[36] In the years prior to the Reformation, information given to a priest during the confessional was privileged from disclosure in a court of law. Sir Edmund Coke argued that the privilege survived the Reformation. And in some later cases judges showed themselves willing to intervene to stop a clergyman from being forced to testify. In *Broad v Pitt* (1828) Best CJ said that 'I for one will never compel a clergyman to disclose communications to him by a prisoner, but if he chooses to disclose them I shall receive them in evidence.'[37]

In *R v Griffin* (1853)[38] the prosecution in a murder case sought to adduce evidence of conversations which had taken place between the defendant and the workhouse chaplain. Alderson B said that the conversations should not be given in evidence. He said that the principle here was the same as that in the lawyer–client relationship. If the chaplain were forced to give evidence, defendants would be left without prior spiritual assistance because they would be so frightened of disclosure that they would not be willing to come forward for help. However, in many other cases the courts have propounded the view that no priest–penitent privilege exists in English law. Cross suggests that both judicial authority and textbook writers are against the existence of the privilege.[39] Noakes has also written that there is a 'formidable set of dicta' against the existence of a priest–penitent privilege, although he puts forward the view that the existence of the privilege can be seen still as an open question.[40]

Were the courts to hold that a clergy privilege did exist, this would indeed provide a sharp contrast to the rejection in case-law of the doctor–patient privilege. It would amount to the exclusion of evidence on grounds of policy unrelated to the considerations of the administration of justice which underpins the rest of the exclusionary rules of privilege and public interest which we have considered. Finally, if privilege protection were extended to the doctor–patient relationship, some thought might have to be given to whether the role the clergy in pastoral counselling also requires protection.

In only one situation has statutory recognition been given directly to the need to protect confidential information in the litigation process. That is where the individual in question is a journalist. Prior to 1982, if a journalist refused to answer questions in court about his sources of information, the judge could find him in contempt of court just as he can hold a doctor in contempt of court for his refusal to answer questions put to him by counsel. Now the Contempt of Court Act 1981 provides in section 10 that:

> No court may require a person to disclose nor is any person guilty of contempt for failure to disclose the source of information in a publication for which he is responsible unless it is established to the satisfaction of the court that disclosure is necessary in the interests of justice or national security for the prevention of disorder or crime.

This section does not introduce an absolute legal privilege for either the sources of the journalist's information or the journalist himself. At common law the courts firmly rejected such a privilege, as was confirmed by the House of Lords in *British Steel v Granada Television* (1981).[41]

Section 10 is limited to requiring disclosure in situations where it is necessary in the interests of justice, national security and the prevention of crime. The extent to which the confidentiality of journalists' sources will be protected is dependent upon judicial interpretation of this section. As far as national security is concerned, if this is pleaded it is unlikely that a claim by a journalist to preserve the confidentiality of his sources will succeed. The courts have always been reticent to challenge claims of 'national security'. In the only case so far decided on this particular issue raised by section 10, the House of Lords held that disclosure of a photostat copy of a memo which had been leaked to the *Guardian* was justified in the interests of national security.[42]

The exception of what amounts to the 'prevention of crime' was considered in the case of *Re an Investigation under the Company Securities (Insider Dealing) Act 1985* (1988).[43] This case concerned the interpretation of a comparable clause to that of section 10 contained in the Insider Dealing Act 1985. In the House of Lords, Lord Griffiths, with whom Lord Goff agreed, held that the words 'prevention of crime' went far beyond prevention of an individual crime and referred to crime and disorder as a threat to society at large. Lord Oliver however, was, more circumspect. He agreed that the phrase went far beyond the need to investigate a particular individual crime. But it was not enough simply to say that disclosure was necessary for the detection of a particular crime: something more was required. On the facts of the case he thought that the onus had been narrowly discharged.

It is unlikely that the courts will in the future use section 10 as a broad protection for journalists. This was emphasised in a recent case – that of *X v Morgan Grampian Publishers* (1990).[44] This case concerned William Goodwin, a trainee reporter on a specialist magazine, *The Engineer*. He was rung one morning by a person who gave him information relating to the business affairs of a company whose name remains secret. The reporter wrote an article about the company, but its publication was stopped by injunction. The firm argued that sensitive financial information had been stolen. They took steps to recover Goodwin's notes, which, it was claimed, would enable the thief to be identified. Goodwin decided that he owed an obligation to his source and remained silent. The court took the view that his professional ethical obligation alone could not avail him and that if he did not disclose the information as required, he could (as he ultimately was) be held to be in contempt of court and fined. The House of Lords, considering the exception of the interests of justice, gave a broad interpretation of the concept. As Lord Oliver held:

> The interest of the public in the administration of justice must, in my opinion, embrace its interest in the maintenance of a system of law within the framework of which every citizen has the ability and the freedom to exercise his legal right to remedy any wrong done to him or to prevent it being done whether or not through the medium of legal proceedings.[45]

At present, then, confidentiality by itself is no ground for resisting disclosure in a court of law. The ethical obligation owed by doctor to patient may be important, but a strong ethical justification by itself is no reason to keep quiet in the courtroom. Are we undervaluing confidentiality in our society? How vital is it to ensure that the court has full access to all relevant evidence? Might that interest be overridden in some situations? Other nations have been far less reticent about affording privilege protection to medical confidentiality.

CONTRAST AND COMPARISON: MEDICAL PROFESSIONAL PRIVILEGE IN OTHER LANDS

The doctor–patient relationship has been the subject of privilege protection in various nations, and in jurisdictions where the privilege is absent there has been active consideration of whether such a privilege should be introduced.

United States

While in England confidentiality of itself has been decisively rejected as the basis of a privilege, in the United States the well-known American jurist Wigmore[46] regarded confidentiality as a vitally important consideration in determining whether a particular privilege should be enacted. Wigmore suggested that claims that a privilege should be granted be subject to a four-part test:

1 Communications must originate in confidence that they will not be disclosed.
2 The element of confidentiality must be essential to the satisfactory maintenance of the relationship between the parties.
3 The relationship must be one which should be sedulously fostered.
4 The injury caused to the relationship by the disclosure of the communication must be greater than the benefit gained by the correct disposal of litigation.

Wigmore was himself opposed to the doctor–patient privilege on the grounds that it did not satisfy these four criteria. He argued that only in a very few cases are facts communicated to a doctor in any real sense 'confidential': most of the time people are willing to discuss their ailments freely with other people. He argued that communications to a doctor would continue to be made regardless of the existence of a privilege. Wigmore's approach has been criticised in the States, and there have been commentators, as we shall see later, who are prepared to argue that absence of a privilege may indeed have the effect of deterring those wanting medical help.

Despite Wigmore's opposition, there is extensive doctor–patient privilege protection in many states of the USA. Long before Wigmore wrote his treatise on evidence, the New York Privilege Statute of 1828 provided that

> No person authorised to practice physic or surgery shall be
> allowed to disclose any information which he may have acquired

in attending a patient in a professional character and which information was necessary for him to prescribe for such a patient as a physician or to do any act for him as a surgeon.

Forty states in the USA now have some form of privilege protection. But in some states the privilege was found to have an undesirably wide scope, and as a result there was an erosion of the privilege by both judiciary and legislature. Criticism of a general doctor–patient privilege led to its being excluded from the Federal Rules of Evidence. The Advisory Committee on the Federal Rules of Evidence noted that 'while many states have by statute created the privilege, the exceptions which have been found necessary in order to avoid fraud are so numerous as to leave little if any basis for the privilege.'[47]

There has been a far more favourable response to suggestions that privilege protection be granted to the psychiatrist–patient relationship. This is partly in response to the very strong lobby by those involved in the practice of psychotherapy and psychiatry in the United States. The first American case involving the psychiatrist–patient privilege was the Grinker case.[48] Dr Roy Grinker senior refused to testify about his patient in an alienation of affection case brought by his patient's husband. He claimed that he was entitled to privilege because confidentiality was a prerequisite of the therapeutic relationship. The judge held that the psychiatrist–patient relationship was worthy of protection and ruled in Grinker's favour. The case was not a formal legal precedent, but it was followed both in subsequent litigation and by a number of states enacting psychiatric privilege protection. It is often crucial that confidentiality be preserved in psychiatric medical practice, and in recognition of this the Federal Rules of Evidence originally incorporated a psychotherapist–patient privilege,[49] but this rule was not adopted by Congress. Despite this rejection of a general privilege rule there has been some recognition of psychiatrist/psychotherapist privilege in Federal cases. Rule 501 of the Federal Rules of Evidence provides that other than as is provided by the US Constitution, Acts of Congress or Rules of the Supreme Court, the existence of privilege shall be determined by the principles of the common law. The arguments advanced by the Supreme Court in relation to Rule 504 have been used by the courts in determining whether a psychiatrist–patient privilege exists in Federal common law.[50]

The theoretical foundation upon which the doctor–patient evidential privilege is based has been the subject of considerable discussion in the United States. There has been a movement away from the utilitarian balancing test of Wigmore towards the idea that the privilege should be justified on the basis of the patient's fundamental human right to privacy.[51] It has also been argued that the patient is entitled to privilege protection for his medical information by virtue of his constitutional right to privacy. This is the rationale behind privilege protection in three states: Pennsylvania, California and Alaska.

Canada

In Canada no common-law medical professional privilege developed, and the legislatures of the various provinces have been unwilling to follow their near neighbours in the United States. Only Quebec has a privilege statute.[52] This provides that communications made in confidence to priests, advocates, physicians and dentists cannot be disclosed unless authorised expressly or impliedly by those who confided in them.[53] The Canadian courts have, however, been concerned to safeguard confidential information. There has been some debate as to whether there is a judicial discretion to exclude confidential information, and if there is such a discretion, what form it takes. In *Dembie v Dembie* (1963)[54] Stewart J held that it was shocking that one profession should dictate the ethics of another and refused to order a psychiatrist to testify. In *Cronkwright v Cronkwright* (1970)[55] Wright J held that a clergyman who had attempted the reconciliation of a married couple could not claim privilege. But he went on to say that persons enjoying confidences and professional people needed special protection and that the judge possessed a discretion to exclude confidential professional information. In reaching his decision, however, Wright J was relying upon the decision of the Ontario Court of Appeal in *R v Wray* (1970).[56] This case had actually been overturned just before his judgment had been delivered in the Supreme Court of Canada, but the court were not aware of that more recent decision.[57] The court held that the trial judge could exercise his discretion only if the admission of the evidence would be unfair. To admit relevant evidence of probative value was not unfair. This was followed in *In Reference re Legislative Privilege* (1978),[58] where the Ontario Court of Appeal held that 'there is no recognised discretion to exclude relevant and admissible evidence based on confidentiality alone'.[59]

Two Canadian law reform bodies have examined this question of whether the physician–patient relationship should be accorded an evidential privilege in the context of a general review of the subject of professional privilege. The Canadian Law Reform Commission in their study paper No. 12 pointed out some of the problems in enacting a privilege for the medical profession.[60] For example how does one determine what is and what is not 'confidential'? Some ailments may be of a more sensitive and controversial nature than others. Patients who suffer from illnesses which require treatment by means of psychiatry or psychotherapy require a higher degree of confidentiality than those suffering from certain physical ailments. The report concluded, however, that a judicial discretion should be established by statute to give the court power to exclude certain professionals from being compelled to testify regarding the confidences of their clients. A judge could refuse to force a witness to give evidence if, first, he believed it to be unfair or inequitable to compel him to disclose facts confided to him in the exercise of his profession, or which had been divulged to the professional for the purposes of obtaining professional assistance, and second, if he believed that the prejudice caused by the disclosure would be greater than the benefit which the administration of justice might derive from such disclosure.

The generally favourable response of the Canadian Law Reform Commission to a claim for special protection must be contrasted with that of the Federal Provincial Task Force on the Uniform Rules of Evidence.[61] This Committee totally rejected the introduction of a privilege for professional relationships. In their view the public interest in the administration of justice outweighed the public interest in the protection of confidentiality. A privilege could have the effect of misleading the tribunal if highly probative facts were suppressed and could deprive a party to the case of the ability to put the whole truth before the court. The existing law was in their view quite adequate. If new privileges were needed, then the courts were capable of evolving these when the need arose. They referred to the case of *Slavutych v Baker* (1975),[62] in which the Supreme Court of Canada had held that judges could examine the merits of arguments both for and against the creation of new privileges for confidential communications. The court gave judicial recognition to Wigmore's four-part test. In one limited situation they saw a doctor–patient privilege as being justified; that of communications between a defendant and a psychiatrist when these formed part of a court-ordered psychiatric examination. This was regarded as being in the public interest in encouraging more accurate fact finding in the hearing concerning the defendant's fitness to plead. One of the Committee members, Kenneth Chasee, dissented from the findings of the majority. He argued that a psychotherapist–patient privilege should be enacted protecting all communications between therapist and patient subject to three exceptions. The privilege would not apply if, first, the court proceedings were for hospitalisation, or second, the examination had taken place after an order made by a judge, or third, the accused had put his mental or emotional condition in issue. At present none of these recommendations have been enacted.

Australia and New Zealand

In Australia the states of Victoria, Tasmania and Northern Territory have expressly recognised a privilege protecting the physician–patient relationship.[63] The evidential privileges which apply in all these states take a substantially similar form and apply only in civil proceedings. The Evidence Act 1910 of Victoria provides, for example, in section 96 (2) that

> No physician or surgeon shall without the consent of his patient divulge in any civil action or proceeding, unless the sanity of or the testamentary capacity of the patient is the matter in dispute, any information which he has acquired in attending the patient and which was necessary to enable him to prescribe or act for the patient.

The Australian Law Reform Commission have, like their Canadian counterparts, considered the question of professional privilege.[64] They recommended that the court should have a general discretion to protect communications/records made in circumstances in which one party is under an obligation not to disclose them. The court should first consider if disclosure is likely to cause harm to an interested person; so, for example, if the psychiatrist's revelation in court would harm the individual patient, that evidence could be excluded. Alternatively, even if disclosure did not cause harm to that particular person, but the disclosure could cause harm to the doctor–patient relationship, then again the court may exclude it. Third, if the disclosure would harm relationships of the type concerned, then evidence may be excluded. In a situation in which a psychiatrist was to testify about the condition of his patient, the court could thus take into account the effect which enforced disclosure would have on psychiatrist–patient relationships in general. After deciding that harm may result from the disclosure the Commission proposed that the judge in the case should then assess whether the harm outweighed any merit in the evidence being admitted. In making this assessment the judge would take into account a number of variables such as the importance of the evidence in the proceedings and the extent to which the contents of the communication or the document had been already disclosed. These recommendations were incorporated in their Evidence Bill 1987. Australia's near neighbour New Zealand introduced a medical professional privilege as early as 1968.[65] It was not until 1980, however that any extension of the privilege was made to criminal proceedings. The privilege is limited in scope. This is because the policy behind it was that some illnesses, addictions and forms of behaviour should not be the subject of prosecution. To come within the statute the communications between doctor and patient must have been in order to enable the doctor to examine and act for the patient for (a) drug dependency or (b) any other condition or behaviour which manifests itself in criminal conduct.

Thus other jurisdictions have already ventured into fields where English law reformers fear to tread. This book does not have the scope to examine the argument that privilege protection should be extended to all professional confidences, but the doctor–patient relationship is an important relationship of confidence, and it should not be forgotten that a doctor is liable to be disciplined by his own professional body for breach of confidences entrusted to him by his patient.

But while medical confidentiality may be a value which you believe should be upheld in the courtroom, does that mean we really need to go as far as some other jurisdictions? Are there other equally efficient methods of protecting doctor–patient confidences in the courtroom without going as far as full privilege protection?

WHY A PRIVILEGE AT ALL?

Millions of people consult their doctors every year, and there appears to be no mass abstention from medical treatment because of fear that doctors will divulge confidential information about them. Our newspapers are not full of accounts of doctors being sent to jail because their conscience informs them that they must not break confidence and give evidence. Why, then, if the present system is working perfectly adequately, should we disturb the status quo? For one thing, some might want to argue that the present system provides adequate safeguards limiting the disclosure of sensitive personal information.

One of these safeguards is that of the discretion of the judge to exclude evidence. In *Attorney General v Mulholland* (1963),[66] Lord Denning indicated that the judge had some form of discretion to exclude confidences. In that case two journalists claimed that they were entitled to refuse to give a Tribunal of Inquiry examining the Vassall Spy case details of their sources of information. The court rejected their claim that their status as journalists entitled them to refuse to testify. Lord Denning said that

> The judge will respect the confidences which each member of these honourable professions [the doctor or the clergyman or the banker] receives in the course of it and will not direct them to answer unless not only is it relevant but also it is a proper and indeed necessary question in the course of justice to be put and answered. A judge is the person entrusted, on behalf of the community, to weigh these conflicting interests – to weigh on the one hand the respect due to confidence in the profession and on the other hand the ultimate interest of the community in justice being done, or in a case of a tribunal such as this, in a proper investigation being made into these serious allegations. If a judge determine that the journalist should answer then no privilege shall avail them to refuse.[67]

Since that case, however, considerable scepticism has surrounded claims of a judicial discretion. The Law Reform Committee in their report on the law of evidence in civil proceedings said that such a discretion already existed allowing the judge to exclude evidence where, for instance, disclosure would be a breach of some ethical or social value and non-disclosure would be unlikely to result in serious injustice in the particular case.[68] In their later report the Criminal Law Revision Committee, commenting upon the Law Reform Committee, expressed considerable doubts as to whether a judge could ever exclude a witness from answering a relevant question asked by the defence on the grounds that in answering it the witness would be committing a breach of confidence.[69]

The scope of the judicial discretion to exclude evidence was the subject of some discussion by the House of Lords in the case of *D v NSPCC* in the context of civil litigation. Lord Hailsham cited the Law Reform Committee's report, which suggested that such a discretion was in existence, and said that this represented the law in 1967.[70] Yet despite this he later appeared to contradict himself and to reject the existence of a general discretion. Another member of the House of Lords, Lord Simon, said that the notion of a judicial discretion was not supported in the case-law, nor was it desirable in principle. In his view the true position was that the judge could only rule as to whether the medical evidence was admissible. However, the judge did have some power in the form of moral authority. He could ask counsel whether he felt it really necessary to press the question if in the circumstances there was a strong ethical and professional inhibition against answering it. But he concluded with the memorable words: 'But it is far from the exercise of a formal discretion. And if it comes to the forensic crunch it must be law not discretion which is in command.'[71]

Lord Edmund Davies also doubted the existence of such a wide discretion.[72] He noted that Lord Denning in *Attorney General v Mulholland* had held that the only profession which had been granted a privilege was the legal profession. But he then went on to say that evidence could be excluded on public-policy grounds if a confidential relationship existed and if disclosure would be in breach of some ethical or social value involving the public interest. In the civil case of *Re C*[73] which is the most recent case involving disputed admission of medical evidence and which was discussed earlier in the context of the public-policy exclusionary rule, the court took the approach that they did have a judicial discretion to exclude medical evidence. However, they held that on the facts of that case the evidence in question should be admitted in a case which concerned the important issue of the welfare of a child.

As far as criminal litigation is concerned, while the courts have long recognised the existence of a discretion to exclude evidence, there has been some dispute about its scope. In *R v Sang* (1980),[74] the House of Lords held that the judge has a discretion to refuse to admit what would otherwise be legally admissible evidence, if in his opinion the prejudicial effect outweighs the probative value and in certain situations relating to admissions and confessions where the evidence has been obtained improperly or unfairly. The exact extent of this discretion was, however, left somewhat uncertain, with various members of the House of Lords expressing the discretion in different ways.[75] This common-law discretion has never been used to exclude evidence simply on grounds of breach of confidence. One case in which medical evidence was excluded was *R v Payne* (1963).[76] In that case it was held that evidence of a medical examination would be excluded where the examination had been carried out by a doctor, the patient being assured that the results obtained would not be used in evidence. The reason why evidence was excluded in this case was that it would be unfair to admit the evidence, not that it was confidential. The use of judicial discretion to exclude confidential information in this manner was later criticised by Viscount Dilhorne in *Sang*.[77]

While the common-law discretion was expressly preserved by section 82 (3) of the Police and Criminal Evidence Act 1984, the courts appear to be concentrating upon use of the new statutory discretion contained in section 78 of that Act.

Section 78 of the Police and Criminal Evidence Act 1984 provides that:

> (1) In any proceedings the court may refuse to allow evidence on which the prosecution wishes to rely to be given if it appears to the court, having regard to all the circumstances, including the circumstances in which the evidence was obtained, the admission of the evidence would have such an adverse effect on the fairness of the proceedings that the court should not admit it.

This section has been used by the courts to enable them to exclude evidence from a trial typically in a situation in which evidence had been obtained in contravention of the codes of practice relating to police investigation. In *R v McDonald* (1990),[78] however, statements were made to the effect that the section may have a broader scope.

In this case the prosecution sought to put before the court a report made by a psychiatrist who had examined the defendant. The defendant objected, saying that the report of conversations which had taken place was confidential. He argued that the evidence would have an adverse effect on the fairness of his trial and that the judge should use his discretion under section 78 to exclude this evidence. The judge at first instance rejected his claim, and his decision was upheld in the Court of Appeal.

In the Court of Appeal, Stuart Smith LJ said that section 78 required the judge to determine whether evidence should be admitted on the basis not of whether it had been obtained unfairly but of whether it had been used unfairly. This question was one for the judge to decide acting upon the facts of an individual case. In the present case the first-instance judge had exercised his discretion correctly. But his Lordship went on to say that it was only on rare occasions or in exceptional circumstances that the prosecution would seek to adduce evidence of what a defendant had said to his doctor if the issue before the court was non-medical. The claim of exclusion was not successful here, but statements of the Court of Appeal appear to indicate that section 78 may have some scope in the exclusion of medical evidence from the courtroom. Section 78 has already been used far more extensively than was first thought when the 1984 Act was passed,[79] but use of this section to exclude medical evidence in the future is undesirable. The section was largely a response to the problem of whether to exclude evidence obtained illegally; it was surely not an attempt totally to rewrite the law relating to exclusion of evidence to enable the judiciary to exercise their conscience to exclude medical evidence.

It is undesirable for a judicial discretion enabling the exclusion of medical evidence to evolve through *ad hoc* judicial development. Unchecked discretion may fail to take into account adequately the fact that not all patient information may be worthy of protection in the courtroom. One area of health-care practice in which a blanket exclusionary rule would appear to be far more appropriate than an uncertain discretion is that of psychiatric medicine, which, as we shall see, is highly confidential in nature. This information is so sensitive that some might argue that it may be undesirable for admission of that evidence to depend on any form of balancing test or for that matter for confidence to be broken by the judiciary being able to review that evidence to determine whether it should be admitted as evidence.

The second way in which the confidentiality of patients' disclosures to their doctors can be safeguarded at present is by the hearing being conducted *in camera*. This refers to the power of the judge to close the court, to remove persons from the public gallery and to continue the hearing in private. In *Scott v Scott*[80] Viscount Haldane held that the crucial issue was the need to ensure the efficient administration of justice. The public may be removed from certain types of hearings in the interests of protecting the privacy of those concerned.

For example, section 37 of the Children and Young Persons Act 1933 provides that the judge can clear the court when children are giving evidence in cases involving conduct contrary to decency or morality. The advantage of hearings *in camera* is that they enable evidence to be given, but with the minimum of infringement of individual confidentiality, especially if coupled with the power of the court to impose restrictions upon the reporting of proceedings. But is this a satisfactory method of compromise in all cases? In the United States it has been suggested that the journalist–source privilege which had been enacted in one state did not apply to *in camera* hearings.[81] The view advanced in this case has been supported by Westen, who has argued that as far as most privileges are concerned the court can compel a witness to disclose his evidence *in camera*.[82] However, Hill suggests that whether *in camera* hearings are satisfactory depends on the particular privilege in question:[83] 'Obviously this cannot be a principle of general application. Thus coerced disclosure *in camera* would hardly be consistent with the privilege against self-incrimination or the priest–penitent privilege.'[84] I suggest that *in camera* hearings would in many situations not be a suitable solution to the problem of protecting doctor–patient confidences. The doctor's obligation would be overridden by the disclosure having to take place in the courtroom situation, and this breach of obligation would be as fundamental whether disclosure was made behind closed doors or in open court.

Confidentiality is then a value much underrated in the law of evidence. Should there be more protection for doctor–patient confidences in the courtroom? While there is no evidential privilege as such, there may be room for argument concerning the extent to which a judicial discretion to exclude certain confidential information exists. In addition the judge of course has the power to press counsel gently not to pursue a line of questioning. The present situation is uncertain and unsatisfactory. Professional confidentiality in the courtroom requires re-examination. Much has been made of the need to ensure that in a court of law all relevant and admissible evidence is adduced, but are there not other values which need to be pursued and which may on occasion outweigh considerations of the efficient administration of justice? These are the issues to which we turn in the next chapter.

3

CONFIDENTIALITY: A PRINCIPLE TO BE PROTECTED?

The patient is at present unable to stop his personal medical information being disclosed in the courtroom. In the last chapter we saw that to claim simply that the information was 'confidential' is not enough in English law. Other jurisdictions, however, have protected confidential medical information through the use of professional privilege. But should we also go along that road? The patient may think that his information is crucially confidential, but should the law take any notice of that claim? Just what is so important about confidential information? In those jurisdictions where medical privilege has been granted, two strands of ethical reasoning have been used to justify courtroom confidentiality. The first is utilitarianism; the second is a deontological argument involving the natural or human right to privacy.

There is a major problem in resorting to philosophical theory as a basis for an evidential privilege. Ethical reasoning provides us with the tools for analysis, but in the end we have to make our own choices. There is no consensus as to priorities among ethical values. In this chapter I seek to examine the advantages and disadvantages of two theoretical approaches – utilitarianism and a rights-based argument – both of which have been used in support of a professional privilege protecting confidential information. I suggest that of these two arguments a human rights argument based upon the patient's right to privacy is preferable. But philosophical justifications must also be tempered by legal reality. While adopting a balancing test of countervailing human rights, we need to remain aware that rights are on occasion overborne by other interests such as public-policy considerations.

UTILITARIANISM

There have been many attempts to take utilitarianism out of the realms of philosophical abstraction and to apply its principles to problems which exist in society. One of the most famous was that of Jeremy Bentham. In his work *The Principles of Morals and Legislation* he made use of utilitarian analysis in suggesting reforms to the legal system.[1] The writings of Bentham form the starting point of my discussion here. First some general points about utilitarianism. The theory developed as a reaction to natural-law reasoning. Utilitarians reject the notion that it is possible to derive principles of morality by means of intuition, arguing that they can only be ascertained by means of empirical research. It is a combination of two approaches, the consequentialist approach, namely that the rightness of an action is determined by reference to its consequences, and the hedonistic approach, namely that the only thing which is good in itself is pleasure and the only thing that is bad in itself is pain. The core concept of the theory is that of 'utility'. Utility is maximised if following one course of conduct has a greater chance of augmenting the happiness of the community than diminishing it.

In deciding when this point was reached Bentham suggested that the legislator should use what he termed a 'felicific calculus' of pleasure and pain. If a course of conduct produced a preponderance of pleasure over pain, then utility would be maximised. In undertaking this calculation the legislator was to use certain variables, to identify the weight of each individual pleasure and pain. These variables were the intensity of the pleasure and pain, the certainty of its occurring and its propinquity. The utility of taking one course of action could then be compared with the utility of taking another course of action.

This basic form of utilitarian analysis is referred to as 'act utilitarianism': the agent seeking to determine his actions by reference to utility must decide the utility of each action separately. Later writers developed more sophisticated versions of the theory.[2] I propose to discuss briefly the work of one such writer, J. S. Mill. The foundations of Mill's theory are essentially Benthamite, but there are significant differences between them. In his essay *Utilitarianism*, Mill begins by defining utilitarianism in terms very similar to those used by Bentham:[3] 'The creed which accepts utility as the foundation of morality holds actions to be right in proportion to their tendency to promote happiness and wrong in their tendency to promote unhappiness.'[4] Happiness according to Mill was to be regarded as pleasure, while unhappiness was to be regarded as pain, the deprivation of pleasure. Having begun his analysis by drawing parallels with Benthamite theory, Mill strikes out on his own. One of the major criticisms of Bentham's theory was that it was wrong to say that life had no higher end than mere pleasure. In suggesting such a goal it was argued that Bentham was demeaning mankind by equating humans with the animals, who, it was said, had no higher goal than pleasure. Mill argued that such criticism ignored the fact that there are different types of pleasure. Some types of pleasure were more desirable, more valuable, than others. Mill said that those who are equally acquainted with and equally capable of enjoying both give a more marked preference to those which employ their higher faculties. Mill distinguished the lower from the higher pleasures by saying that while the former were characterised by the fact that they involve bodily sensations and are almost universally enjoyed, the latter are pleasures of the intellect and require much effort and skill for pleasure to be gained from them, but once pleasure is gained, it lasts far longer than the lower pleasures.

It has been suggested that the main differences between Bentham and Mill lay in the manner in which they computed utility. Ormston, for example, suggests that Mill was a rule utilitarian.[5] Instead of calculating utility in each situation before he follows a particular course of action as with basic utilitarian analysis, a rule utilitarian will refer to a rule of conduct to guide his action in a particular situation. This rule will be decided by reference to utility. The difference between these approaches can be seen best by using an example. A doctor is dealing with a patient who is HIV positive. The patient has not told his girlfriend that he has the virus. The doctor debates whether he should inform the girlfriend. He decides to act by reference to utility. If he is an act utilitarian, he will estimate the 'pleasures' which will result from keeping the patient's confidences, such as the importance of ensuring that his patient is not discouraged from coming forward for treatment. He will assess the 'pains', such as the potential harm which may well accrue to the girlfriend if he decides to keep the patient's confidences, and will balance these against each other. If he is a rule utilitarian, he will decide whether or not to keep the patient's confidence by following a rule of conduct which has itself been decided by reference to utility. This general rule will be determined by a very similar calculation to that of act-utilitarian analysis, but instead of considering the harm which may accrue to particular individuals, he will take more general considerations into account, such as the harm which could be caused to doctor–patient relationships as a whole if patients were aware that their doctors routinely disclosed confidential information.

J. J. C. Smart has argued that act and rule utilitarianism are not totally different creatures.[6] If a conflict arises between two rules which have been derived from a calculation of utility, the moral agent will be left to calculate which rule will maximise utility in a particular situation. Those who regard rule utilitarianism as a separate theory regard Mill as the leading exponent.[7] Others, such as Mabbott, have suggested that Mill himself was none too sure of the difference between the approaches and that although in some passages he appears to be a rule utilitarian, in other passages he lapses into act utilitarianism.[8] I agree with the scepticism of Smart regarding rule utilitarianism and that rule utilitarianism ultimately does collapse into act utilitarianism. I do not therefore propose to use rule-utilitarian analysis to determine whether utilitarianism is a satisfactory justification for an evidential privilege. But should act utilitarianism be used? Is it appropriate as a basis for an exclusionary rule of evidence? After all, the high priest of utilitarianism, Jeremy Bentham, was highly critical of such rules: 'the principle of exclusion is bad by its effects and its tendency; it encourages every hurtful disposition because it increases the possibility of being unjust'.[9]

The admission of evidence according to Bentham was to be a matter for the judge, who was to have a wide exclusionary discretion. Wherever possible, though, evidence was to be admitted and exclusion of evidence should only take place if the evidence was irrelevant or superfluous or because allowing it to be admitted would cause preponderant vexation and delay. Was Bentham in his writings blinded by subconscious prejudice? Twining has suggested that Bentham's approach could be biased by influences in his formative years.[10] He recounts how Bentham aged 11 or 12 read a best-seller called *An Apology for the Conduct of Mrs T. C. Phillips*. The book told the life story of Teresa Constantia Phillips, who had been reformed from her earlier life as a prostitute by marriage to a Dutch merchant, but, after her marriage was annulled, suffered eventual ruin through her efforts to vindicate her rights in court. Twining notes that

> The sad tale of Mrs Phillips contained many of the ingredients that he was later to attack in the technical system of procedure, interminable delays, multiple jurisdictions; obfuscating

41

technicalities; exclusion of relevant evidence; exclusion of parties (and others) as witnesses; the tolerance of chicanery and perjury; abuse of religion and above all appalling expense arising from the financial interests of lawyers and officials who were responsible for prolonging and complicating legal proceedings.[11]

Bentham's writings presuppose that the greatest happiness is best achieved by the fullest fact-finding process compatible with resolution of disputes within a reasonable time. Detailed calculation could well, however, reveal that the greatest happiness was achieved instead by some value such as that of confidentiality being given protection, even if this is at the expense of the court being debarred access to certain evidence.

It could be argued that a utilitarian test has already been used in the law of evidence but that this provides no joy for those who advocate this as a basis for a medical professional privilege. The test which could be cited is that of Wigmore, writing in the United States.[12] Wigmore suggested that before a relationship was accorded privilege protection it should be subjected to a four-part test, and only if it satisfied all the limbs of that test should the relationship be given privilege.[13] The four criteria were:

1 Communications between the parties had to originate in a confidence that they would not be disclosed.
2 The elements of confidentiality must be essential to the full and satisfactory maintenance of the relationship between the parties.
3 The relationship was one which in the opinion of the community ought to be sedulously fostered.
4 The injury that would inure to the relationship by the disclosure of the communication must be greater than the benefit gained through the correct disposal of litigation.

Wigmore argued strenuously that the medical professional privilege did not fit this test. The doctor–patient relationship did not have to be fostered by the existence of an evidential privilege, he argued; and there was no evidence that the presence or absence of a privilege made any appreciable difference to the numbers of patients who went forward to seek treatment.

It is submitted that this rejection of privilege protection by Wigmore does not sound the death knell of utilitarian analysis. Wigmore's test is some considerable way from the theoretical utilitarian approach advocated by philosophers. Throughout his discussion he assumes that confidentiality is a value which is important but fails to provide any support for this view. In the fourth part of this test he provides what may be regarded as a crude utilitarian test of benefits versus disadvantages. But when using the test Wigmore makes what are in essence subjective assertions. This is a far cry from Bentham's scientific analysis. It is possible to reject Wigmore's largely rhetorical rejection of medical professional privilege while at the same time arguing in favour of a utilitarian-based privilege justification.

We are still left, though, with the question, is utilitarianism the most satisfactory philosophical foundation for the privilege to rest upon? The problems which are posed by an application of utilitarian analysis are formidable. To determine whether utility is maximised in this context would be an exceedingly complex task. Some of the difficulties which would arise can best be illustrated by outlining the type of empirical investigation which would be needed under an 'act-utilitarian' test.

The prospective legislator who wanted to use such a test would need to calculate the 'pleasures' which would result from enacting a privilege and to balance them against the 'pains' that it would bring. A sceptic might want to argue at this point that it is surely being overly simple to talk of 'pleasures' and 'pains' in this context. An individual may get pleasure from a good book, a splendid dinner, spectacular scenery, but from an evidential privilege? It is suggested that there are some 'pleasures' which could be derived from enacting such an evidential privilege. Patients may be willing to confide in their medical practitioner secure in the knowledge that their confidences will be kept. Trust between doctor and patient will be fostered. The patient has confidence in the doctor since he knows that he will be able to trust him. The doctor appreciates that the patient is trusting his professional integrity and knows that this trust is well founded. The patient need not be deterred from going for treatment because of not confiding fully in his doctor. In some foreign jurisdictions the need to ensure that the patient is not deterred from seeking treatment by fear of legal action has been seen as a crucial argument by those who advocate an evidential privilege. Fisher has written that people most in need of assistance will often be those who are most concerned about the prospect of legal action.[14] For example,

The mother with the unmanageable child who fears proceedings in the juvenile courts from removing the child from her custody and who is afraid to consult a social worker, the compulsive kleptomaniac who has repeated suspended sentences or probation for his petty thefts who is afraid to visit a psychiatrist, the dissident married couple in the shadow of divorce proceedings who are afraid to make that last attempt at reconciliation by seeking a marriage counsellor, the chronic recidivist in a correctional institution who is afraid to join group therapy because of what the effect on his future parole of this spontaneous disclosure might be . . . these and many more can be cited as situations in which the absence of confidentiality guaranteed by a psychotherapist privilege will deter those in need from those who might be able to help them.[15]

The pain of the privilege can be regarded as being the potential harm which could result from evidence being excluded from the courtroom. These are the considerations which influenced Bentham's writings. At best such exclusion could impede the fact-finding process at the trial; at worst it could lead to a verdict being given which was wrong, leading in a civil action to grave injustice to one of the parties and in a criminal case possibly to wrongful deprivation of liberty or to a guilty man being set free. The extent of the harm caused by such a privilege would be very much dependent on the precise scope of the privilege which was enacted. More evidence would be removed from court scrutiny if the privilege were absolute, preventing the disclosure of any communications between doctor and patient, rather than if one or both of the parties to the relationship were able to waive it.

How easy would it be in practice for an empirical study to be undertaken? If not absolutely impossible, it is submitted that it would be exceedingly difficult and complex. To determine both the extent to which doctor–patient relationships would be fostered and the harm caused to the administration of justice we would require data to answer some of the following questions. How often are doctors required to testify in court? Is the information which they are required to divulge 'confidential' in its nature? How often are doctors required to testify in court when they are unwilling to do so? If a doctor has been forced to give evidence, what was the effect of his disclosures on his patients? Do such disclosures have an adverse effect on his patient's health? Is the patient as a result of that breach of confidence discouraged from going to any doctor? To what extent does an enforced disclosure have repercussions outside that particular doctor–patient relationship? Is knowledge of the disclosure wide-spread in the community, and are people as a result inhibited from seeking medical treatment?

Such research would be costly and complex and could well prove to be inconclusive. It is highly unlikely that a government would ever provide sufficient funds for such a study, and the nature of the research is not of a type likely to attract private funding. Yet, without such research we will have to rely largely on hypothetical speculation as to whether utility is maximised by such a privilege being enacted. In the past the argument that people are discouraged from going to their doctors for treatment by the absence of a privilege has been the subject of considerable criticism. The American jurist Wigmore argued that

> People would not be deterred from seeking medical help because of the possibility of disclosure in court. If they would, how did they fare in the generations before the privilege came? Is it noted in the medical chronicles that after the privilege was established in New York the floodgates of patronage were let open upon the medical profession and long concealed ailments were then for the first time brought forward to receive the blessings of cure?[16]

Wigmore suggested that more harm than good would accrue from such a privilege. Actions by the relatives of deceased persons claiming benefits due or for damages in compensation for wrongful injury would be frustrated because the privilege would debar access to the deceased person's medical records. Similar criticism was levied at the doctor–patient privilege by Chafee:

> This whole argument, that the privilege is necessary to induce persons to see a doctor, sounds like a philosopher's speculation on how men may logically be expected to behave rather than the result of speculation on how men actually behave. Not a single New England State allows the doctor to keep silent on the witness stand. Is there evidence that any ill or injured person in New England has ever stayed from a doctor's office on that account?[17]

The limited amount of empirical research carried out abroad in those nations which have enacted or have contemplated the enactment of such a privilege gives little joy to those who would argue that patients are deterred from seeking treatment by the absence of a privilege.

45

Take, for example, two studies in Canada.[18] In the first province, Ontario, there was no privilege; in the second province, Quebec, a statute had been enacted creating an evidential privilege. The study showed that there was very little difference in the responses from the two provinces, which suggests that the enactment of the statute in the latter province had led to no major changes in the behaviour of Canadians in seeking medical treatment. In Ontario 200 questionnaires were sent out to 40 psychotherapists to distribute to their patients. Sixty-four were returned; only 19 per cent of the respondents either knew or guessed correctly that there was no privilege. No patient said that he would have sought treatment earlier had he known that a privilege existed. In Quebec 200 questionnaires were again sent out and 70 were eventually returned. Some 59 per cent of the respondents knew or guessed correctly that a privilege was in existence, and only 7 per cent said that they would have sought treatment earlier had they known that a privilege was in existence.

Responses also indicated that the medical profession are by no means unanimous as to whether disclosure in the courtroom would cause harm. In Ontario a questionnaire was sent to 445 psychiatrists practising in Toronto; 81 questionnaires were returned. Forty-two per cent of respondents had been asked to disclose confidential communications in court but of these only 12 per cent had ultimately been required to disclose those communications. Forty-three per cent of therapists were of the view that disclosure in court did cause psychological harm to the patients, and 22 per cent said that patients had ended therapy prematurely because of disclosure. In Quebec the same questionnaire was sent to a sample of 427 psychiatrists, 107 of whom returned them completed. Thirty-five per cent of those who responded had been asked to disclose confidential communications in court, although only 7 per cent were ultimately required to do so. Thirty per cent of those therapists believed that disclosure had caused psychological harm, and some 23 per cent said that therapy had been prematurely terminated as a result.

Those wanting to show that the absence of an evidential privilege had a considerable impact upon the likelihood of patients seeking treatment will derive no comfort from these statistics. A considerable number of patients were not aware of whether a privilege existed at all. There was no real indication that people would have sought treatment earlier if a privilege statute had existed. Only a small proportion of therapists in both states had been forced to disclose confidential information. Of these, relatively small percentages thought that harm had been caused. These surveys also pinpoint another problem facing those trying to establish a utilitarian argument by empirical evidence, namely the difficulty of getting patients and therapists actually to respond. No return rate even reached 50 per cent.

A further complication with the utilitarian approach is the fact that in considering the 'pleasures' and 'pains' of protecting confidential medical information we need to bear in mind that not all patient information is uniformly confidential. Wigmore was of the view that very few ailments could really be regarded as confidential at all: 'Barring the facts of venereal disease and criminal abortion there is hardly a fact in the categories of pathology in which the patient himself attempts to preserve real secrecy. Most of one's ailments are at least explained to intimates.'[19]

While Wigmore's comment may be seen as far too simplistic in an age in which many people seek psychiatric assistance and counselling in the form of psychotherapy, for example, to help face the strains of modern life, it is still true that there are many illnesses which we never treat as 'confidential'. The boundaries of medical confidentiality in modern-day medical practice will be discussed, at length, in the following chapter. It suffices at this stage to note that the many uncertainties in the concept would make it very difficult indeed to pursue a utilitarian analysis.

Alongside these serious practical problems in a utilitarian approach lie questions which have been raised concerning the soundness of the theory itself. It has been argued that we are wrong to suggest that mankind is constantly seeking happiness. G. E. Moore has argued that pleasure is not the sole object of human desire.[20] Our ultimate aim is not pleasure but those things which bring us pleasure. To support his proposition he gives an example of a person who is contemplating drinking a glass of wine. The idea of drinking wine occurs to him and causes an experience of pleasure. This actual felt pleasure causes the desire for a glass of wine to arise. Moore argues that what is desired is the wine, not the actual pleasure thought of in desiring it.

I mentioned earlier that utilitarianism is a consequentialist theory, that is to say, it incorporates the view that the rightness of actions can only be determined by reference to their consequences. According to such an approach, by pledging to keep the confidence of a patient the doctor is not binding himself by an obligation which is absolute, nor, speaking generally, is the obligation to keep one's promises an absolute obligation. They are courses of conduct which should be pursued as long as the 'pleasure' of keeping the obligation is not outweighed by the 'pain' caused by preserving it. But should our choice of conduct always be dependent upon the consequences which may flow from our choice? Are there no absolute values to be pursued, no absolute obligations to be honoured? Bernard Williams has made a powerful attack upon the notion of consequentialism.[21] He argues that certain types of action, or a certain course of conduct, may be the right thing to do even though the consequences which would result would be worse than what would result from not pursuing that course of conduct. Utilitarianism leads to the result, to take an extreme example, that if the greatest happiness of the greatest number of people in a community could be achieved by the removal of a minority of the population, then this should take place, even though such an action could well be morally wrong. An action may have an intrinsic value according to Williams even though it would not pass the greatest happiness test. It could be argued, then, that any utilitarian analysis is inherently flawed because preserving patient confidences is an intrinsically right thing to do, despite the consequences which could result in the form of the harm to the administration of justice.

The fact that the utilitarian approach has been extensively criticised does not mean it should necessarily be abandoned: there are many uncertainties in ethical analysis. But neither does the inherent uncertainty which accompanies any excursion into the realms of ethics justify our unquestioning acceptance of the theory on the grounds that uncertainty is an inevitable price to pay. The flaws in utilitarianism are manifold: not least is the problem of the calculation of which interests are and which are not maximised by utility. I now move to consider the second ethical justification which can be advanced for the protection of medical confidentiality in the court-room, the patient's right to confidentiality.

A RIGHT TO CONFIDENTIALITY

Most people when they feel that they have suffered some wrong are prone to declare that their rights have been infringed. In the area of the doctor–patient relationship claims of rights have proved particularly controversial. In recent years we have heard the claims of 'my right to have an abortion', 'my right to be told of the risks inherent in the operation I am to have'. A patient who finds that his doctor has disclosed medical information about him without his consent is likely to say 'My rights have been infringed'. But such an intuitive reaction that a doctor has been wrong to disclose the information without his patient's consent does not by itself provide sufficiently strong support for an evidential privilege. Instead, what is needed is an analysis of what is meant by the patient's right in this context.

What is a right?

The language of rights has had a very ancient history. As early as the twelfth century, scholars were using the concept of a right in very much the same sense as we use it today: that is to say, to have a right usually meant that one had a 'claim right'.[22] If an individual possessed such a right, it enabled him to demand something of another person. The leading work on the concept of rights in jurisprudence is that of the American scholar Hohfeld, *Fundamental Legal Conceptions*.[23] He suggested that the simple phrase 'P has a right to X' was capable of several meanings. It could refer to the fact that P had no duty not to do X. P in such a situation possessed a privilege. Alternatively, by talking of P's right to do X one could mean that a third person Q had a duty to let P do X. This is the claim right. Third, to say that P had a right to X could mean that he had an ability or power to alter existing legal relations. Finally, Hohfeld argued that the word 'right' could mean that an individual possessed an immunity, that is to say, if P possessed an immunity as regards X, then Q or possibly everyone lacks the power to alter P's legal position as it concerns X.

For the purposes of the rest of this book when I speak of a 'right' I refer to a 'claim right'. The patient, when he says that the doctor owes him a duty to keep his medical information confidential, is asserting that claim right. But if a duty is owed, how did that duty arise, and is the patient correct to argue that it is an enforceable right? There is in English law no duty comparable with that imposed on the medical profession in France, where breach of a patient's confidence is a criminal offence.[24] In the absence of such an existing legal duty we are forced to search for some other duty imposed on the doctor which can be enforced in court.

Rights and human rights

When we refer to fundamental obligations being owed by one person to another it is often in terms of that person's human rights, and the doctor–patient obligation is no exception to this. But just what do we mean by human rights? According to Maurice Cranston, human rights are simply another term for natural rights or the rights of man; natural rights are rights which are capable of being discovered by reference to reason.[25] Margaret MacDonald has written that 'Natural rights, like propositions of natural law generally are not capable of being verified by empirical calculation. They are derived from reason and, are regarded as self-evident.'[26]

Perhaps the point at which natural rights became most influential was during the seventeenth and eighteenth centuries. The theory was used as a catalyst by those who sought political change. Natural-rights theory was linked with the social contract. The natural rights which men possessed formed the basis for their rights as members of society. As Thomas Paine wrote in a famous (or, as some may regard it, notorious) book, *The Rights of Man,* first published in 1791, 'Man did not enter society to become worse than he was before but to have those rights better secured. His natural rights were the foundation of his civil rights.'

Concern about the revolutionary consequences of natural-rights theory along with scepticism regarding the notion of natural law led to some resounding criticism of natural rights in the nineteenth century. Jeremy Bentham, a positivist by legal ideology and a conservative in politics, was vehement in his condemnation:

> Natural rights are simple nonsense; natural and imprescriptable rights, rhetorical nonsense upon stilts. But this rhetorical nonsense ends in the old strain of mischievous nonsense for immediately a list of these pretended natural rights is given and these are so expressed as to present to view legal rights.[27]

For Bentham it was only meaningful to say that a right was in existence if it was a legal right: 'Right and law are correlative terms; as much as son and father. A natural right is a son that never had a father.'

The use of rights in political theory was, Bentham suggested, of no value. If they were regarded as absolute, then they were incompatible with democratic government since they would require total observance. On the other hand, if exceptions were admitted, it would lead to the rights being subject to so many qualifications that they would lose their value. Although Hart suggests that Bentham's vehemence can at least in part be attributed to the fact that he was writing at the height of the Jacobin terror, the opinions he expressed were very influential.[28]

Contemporaneous with Bentham was the parliamentarian Edward Burke.[29] He too poured scathing criticism upon natural rights. While he did not reject totally the language of natural rights he opposed their use as tools for political change. Burke was opposed to any change in the existing social order and saw reliance upon natural rights as a blueprint for political chaos.

Further criticism of natural rights came from another school of thought, different from positivism and lacking the reverence for established authority shown by Burke. For socialist and Marxist theories human rights were the embodiment of what was a 'historical bourgeois individualism'.[30] Socialist writers rejected the view that human rights applied to all people at all times and in all places. In a socialist society people would be working as a community, so there would be no need for individual human rights. Rights were in essence a divisive notion, with each person attempting to pursue his own interest against that of the next person. In a socialist society it was believed that all would be in harmony.

A revival in interest in the concept of inalienable human values has taken place during this century. After the atrocities perpetrated by the Nazi regime during the Second World War a consensus emerged that never again should human beings suffer such gross contempt for their humanity. The post-war period saw the enactment by many states of human-rights declarations. The United Nations drew up its own declarations of human rights, a measure echoed in Europe by the establishment of the European Convention of Human Rights.[31] These declarations were also accompanied by the establishment of enforcement procedures.

Alongside the growing international recognition of human rights there has been a resurgence of interest in jurisprudential theory relating to rights in general and to human rights in particular. John Finnis in his work *Natural Law and Natural Rights* makes a major restatement of natural law-theory.[32] He argues that there are certain basic human values or 'goods' which are self-evidently good. These goods can only be effectively secured through the institution of human law. According to Finnis, law is necessary to create the conditions for a society in which the common good is respected. Moreover it is inherent in one of the basic goods, that of practical reasonableness (this is the good which enables individuals to choose between other basic goods in order to create a coherent plan of life), that we should have respect for the basic value of every act. For Finnis, human rights are basic values which should not be violated.

Interest has also been shown in rights by the political left. I referred above to the scepticism expressed by many authors of socialist theory regarding human rights. Tom Campbell in his book *The Left and Rights* suggests that such rights may not be incompatible with socialism. Campbell sees human rights as protecting important interests which should be secured to all citizens and members of society without regard to divisions such as class, rank, race, sex or nationality. Even though ultimately there may be no need in a socialist society for laws protecting human rights, because such fundamental interests are unlikely to be violated in the ideal socialist community, Campbell argues that this does not exclude the use of such analysis before such a utopia is attained. Several socialist nations have adopted declarations of rights as a response, in Henkins' view, to the growth in human-rights protection elsewhere.[33] But these rights differ from those in Western declarations. They are granted as 'instruments of socialism'. They are not abstract human values but are rights and benefits which the state itself confers as part of life in a socialist society, and they exist and are enjoyed only in so far as they are consistent with socialism. The rights of the citizen, then, are strictly delimited.

If it can be shown that the patient in claiming that his doctor should not testify without his consent is relying upon some fundamental right which was generally respected this would appear to provide us with a strong justification for a privilege. There are certain problems though, that need to be addressed. The first is that of identifying precisely which right we are relying on. Among those who advocate that the existence of natural rights is self-evident there is a significant lack of consensus about which rights are included in the natural-rights category. Historically the number of such rights was seen as limited. Thomas Hobbes regarded the primary right of nature as being that of self-defence.[34]

> That which is not against reason men call right or blameless liberty of using our own natural power and ability. It is therefore a right of nature; that every man may prefer his own life and limbs with all the power he hath.

In contrast John Locke saw the natural rights of man as broader, encompassing rights to life and liberty and a right to property.[35] A still more expansive approach came later. The United States Declaration of Independence proclaimed that all men are created equal and that they are endowed by their creator with certain inalienable rights among which are life, liberty and the pursuit of happiness.[36] Modern rights declarations provide a detailed list of rights outlining rights in the legal process, and rights such as freedom from torture are in essence an expansion upon those expounded by Locke. Also, within the definition of human rights there have been included what are termed 'economic and social rights' such as the right to work and welfare rights such as the right to social security. Criticism of the inclusion of such rights within rights declarations has, however, been made by Maurice Cranston.[37] In his view, for a human right to qualify as such it must be one which is a genuinely universal moral right, and many of these economic and social rights do not fall within this category.

The problem with taking as our starting point some abstract moral right is that it is unlikely to receive acceptance. But if that moral right has already been granted some recognition in law then this would strengthen our hand in using it to support a privilege. Lawyers are more comfortable when there is a legal rule from which they can argue. For the purposes of this book I will make reference to the European Convention of Human Rights. The United Kingdom is a signatory of the Convention. Its provisions, though not directly enforceable in the courts of this country, have been referred to in various judgments. If citizens of the United Kingdom believe that a right to which they are entitled under the Convention has been violated, then they may on receiving no redress for their grievance in the English courts petition the European Commission of Human Rights in Strasbourg.[38] The United Kingdom is required under the Convention to secure to its citizens an adequate remedy if the claim that a violation has occurred is successful. The Convention is cited widely both within the academic world and outside. The use of the Convention for our purposes, is, however, not completely satisfactory. The Convention is drafted very broadly, only a few rights being expressed as absolute, with most rights containing qualifying clauses. Nevertheless, while the Convention is at present not directly enforceable in English courts, it is increasingly providing a point of reference for the judiciary, and frequent mention is made of it in case-law. Does the Convention provide us with a sufficiently strong basis here? Before this issue can be explored, further consideration must be given to which rights we are relying upon.

PRIVACY AND MEDICAL CONFIDENTIALITY

There has been a lively debate upon the parameters of individual privacy in recent years. This interest in the notion of privacy can be regarded as a response to a world in which the individual is increasingly subjected to the scrutiny of others. Although the academic literature upon the subject is usually traced back to the writings of S. Warren and L. Brandeis, in some respects the forerunner of the present discussion is John Stuart Mill. In his essay *On Liberty* Mill argued that persons should be allowed liberty of thought and discussion and also that they should be allowed liberty of action and behaviour.[39] It has been suggested that Mill's writings in this work were influenced by criticism of his own unconventional liaison with Harriet Taylor.[40] Many are of the view that the 1890 *Harvard Law Review* article by Warren and Brandeis[41] was similarly the product of indignation about critical comment concerning the private life of one of the authors. The traditional view is that this article was in part an outraged response to Warren having to suffer the indignity of a report appearing in the local newspaper giving details of his daughter's wedding or the papers having described the family life of the Warrens in great detail. Lewis J. Paper in a biography of Brandeis disputes this, arguing that it is unlikely that Warren's daughter was the cause of any law suits.[42] In 1890, when the article was published, she was only 6 years old and the press coverage of the Warren family life was even by the standards of that day quite tame.

What is quite clearly not in dispute, however, is the fact that the authors had a considerable dislike of the press, which they make evident in their article: 'Instantaneous photographs and newspaper enterprise have invaded the sacred precincts of private and domestic life and numerous mechanical devices threaten to make good the prediction "that what is whispered in the closet shall be proclaimed from the housetops".'[43] They argued that legal recognition of a right to privacy was essential as a means of safeguarding the individual from unwanted intrusions. Brandeis later expressed his concern that privacy should be protected when sitting as a justice of the Supreme Court in *Olmstead v US* and delivering his dissent.[44] The right to privacy was, he argued, our most valuable entitlement, and to safeguard it every unjustifiable intrusion upon the privacy of the individual was to be condemned.

In the years that have followed the Warren and Brandeis article various commentators have put forward what they regard as being embodied in the phrase 'the right to privacy'. Alan Westin, for example, defines privacy as being the claim of individuals and institutions to determine for themselves when, how and to what extent information about themselves is communicated to others.[45] According to Westin, individual privacy has four functions. By maintaining those social processes which safeguard a person's identity, it protects his autonomy. Having autonomy allows individuals to decide for themselves when to 'go public' concerning personal information. Privacy enables a person to gain emotional release from the masks which he wears during everyday life. Third, privacy enables us to undertake self-evaluation. Finally, if individuals are secure in the knowledge of their privacy, then they are able to share their confidences with others.

Westin's approach is akin to that of Charles Fried. He views privacy as essential to secure various fundamental ends or relationships.[46]

> To respect, love, trust, feel affection for others and to regard others as the object of love, trust and affection is at the heart of ourselves as persons among persons and privacy is the necessary atmosphere for these attitudes as oxygen is to combustion.

Love, trust and friendship are according to Fried only possible if persons enjoy and accord to others a certain measure of privacy. The control over information which privacy grants us, Fried suggests, is that which enables us to retain degrees of intimacy. The simple approach to the right to privacy adopted by Warren and Brandeis is developed by Fried, who argues that it does not simply lie in the absence of information being spread about ourselves but justifies our feeling of security in being in control of that information. A further variant upon the approach, which involves treating the control of personal information as inherent in privacy, is provided by William Parent.[47] His definition of privacy is 'the condition of a person not having undocumented personal information known to others'. Parent regards 'personal information' as being information which most people in a given society would not want widely known, facts about which they would say 'it shouldn't be divulged to just anyone', or being facts which certain persons would know are particularly sensitive and do not choose to reveal about themselves. Henkin is one writer who takes a still broader view.[48] He regards privacy as being bound up with the notion of autonomy and the two concepts as not

:ated. This appears to accord with the approach taken to
)f privacy in the United States. There privacy in the form
__.. uver an individual's actions in the private sphere of life has
been recognised. So, for example, the courts have held that privacy
may justify a right to claim access to abortion.[49]

Privacy and confidentiality

The distinction needs to be made at this point between the right to
privacy and the right to confidentiality. An obligation of confidence
arises in a situation in which one person gives information to another
expecting that person to keep that information 'confidential' by not
disclosing it to third parties. The person who imparts the information
binds the recipient by an obligation of confidentiality. Issues of
privacy, however, may arise whether or not we regard the information as 'confidential'. The right to privacy relates to the right of the
individual to control access to his own personal information, and this
does not simply cover information which he has passed on to others
expressly or impliedly expecting them to keep it in confidence. It
applies to all personal information. Individuals have layers of personal information. Some personal information is freely available to
others. Other personal information we regard as private, and as such
we share it with only a limited circle of friends: tastes, interests,
hobbies may come within this category. Within this category is a
further category of personal information which can be seen as
crucially private and personal information. This is information of a
confidential nature. It is confidential information which is especially
worthy of protection. While we should accord protection to all
personal information, that does not mean that all that information is
equally worthy of protection. No one has as far as I am aware ever
claimed that a right to privacy should be regarded as absolute. Where
rights conflict in the courtroom situation, as I will argue below, there
are many weighty interests to be taken into account in conflict with a
general right to present evidence. To claim that an individual should
have the right to exclude all his personal information from the
courtroom is a recipe for proceedings to grind to a standstill. But
where the individual claims that certain information should be
excluded on the grounds of its confidential quality, then the claim of
confidence should be considered seriously and weighed against conflicting rights.

DOES A RIGHT TO CONFIDENTIALITY JUSTIFY A PRIVILEGE?

Medical information is regarded as, if not absolutely confidential, then at the very least, *prima facie* confidential. If, as has been suggested above, the right to privacy incorporates protection of confidential information at its heart then a privilege may be justifiable on the grounds of the patient's right to confidentiality. This would not be the first time that the notion of rights has been used as justification for rules of evidence. The right to privacy has been used to support the enactment of a medical practitioner–patient privilege in the United States.[50] In England and Wales, rights terminology has been invoked to justify both the existence and expansion of rules of evidence. Andrew Ashworth has suggested that the exclusionary rules of evidence excluding evidence unlawfully obtained could best be justified by reference to the rights of the suspect.[51] He argues that the legal system contains certain defined standards for the conduct of criminal investigation and that the citizen has corresponding rights. If those rights were infringed, then evidence obtained as a result of that infringement against the suspect should be excluded – by virtue of what he calls the 'protective principle'. D. J. Galligan has argued that the 'right to silence' of the suspect undergoing criminal investigation can best be justified by reliance upon the individual's right to privacy.[52] The right to silence allows the suspect to protect himself from unwarranted access to his own personal information.

The drawback with a rights-based approach, and one recognised by these writers, is that few rights are ever seen as absolute. I mentioned above that the European Convention has been used to justify the protection of personal information. While this is of some rhetorical importance for the present argument, there are difficulties in relying too heavily upon the provisions of the Convention. While as yet no rule of evidential privilege has been scrutinised under the Convention, were this to be done the Commission and the court would take into account the qualifying provisions of the Convention. Article 8, the article used in recent privacy claims, provides that:

1. Everyone shall have the right to respect for his private and family life his home and correspondence

2. There shall be no interference by a public authority with the exercise of this right except as such as in accordance with the law and is necessary in a democractic society in the interests of

public safety or the economic well-being of the country, for the prevention of disorder or crime, for the protection of health or morals or for the protection of the rights and freedoms of others.

There are, I would suggest, two major countervailing rights and interests which need to be weighed against the right to patient confidentiality developed here. These are the public interest and what can loosely be described as the right to present evidence.

COUNTERVAILING RIGHTS AND INTERESTS

A right to present evidence in the courtroom

While we lack an evidential code to provide us with guidance as to the scope of the law of evidence, which has largely developed *ad hoc* in this country, nevertheless Ian Dennis has written that 'English law acknowledges as fundamental the right of an accused person to a fair trial'.[53] He argues that many of the various rules of evidence in existence at present can be seen as associated with that right. These include the presumption of innocence, the right to silence, the right of an accused person to cross-examine a witness at his trial, the right to have the jury consider his defence as a question of fact in each case and the right not to be put at risk of conviction by evidence the prejudicial effect of which may exceed its probative value. Galligan writes that the accused has a right to procedures which protect against wrongful conviction and punishment, arguing that while these procedures cannot be perfect, they must ensure a level of accuracy in proportion to the importance of the substantive right and to the resources which society can be expected to make available.[54] Rules of evidence can be seen as attempts to regulate evidence which would otherwise if freely admitted create a special risk of a wrongful conviction.

In this book I am not concerned to explore the question of what exactly are the constituent parts of a right to a fair trial. It seems, however, to be generally accepted that part of this right is the right to present all relevant evidence in the courtroom. By this I mean the right not only to call upon one's own witnesses but also to obtain evidence from other persons when that evidence is necessary for one's own case.

Originally witnesses were not compelled to testify in the courtroom. Up to the 1500s the jury acted as both triers of fact and as witnesses, acting on their own local knowledge or searching for evidence before a trial.[55] As time passed it came to be recognised that simple reliance upon the jury was unsatisfactory and that some power to compel the production of witnesses was needed. In 1562–3 a statute of Elizabeth was passed which provided that a penalty would be imposed and a civil action granted against any person who refused to attend after service of process and expenses had been tendered.[56] As Wigmore notes, 'the ordinary witness became by the 1600s the chief source of the jury's information. The notion of a duty was naturally developed from and added to the notion of a freedom or a right.'[57] In 1600 Sir Francis Bacon said that:

> You must know that all subjects without distinction of degrees owe to the King tribute and service, not only of their deed and hand but also of their knowledge and discovery. If there be anything that imports the King's service they ought themselves undemanded to impart it, much more if they be called and examined whether of their own fact or that of others they ought to make direct answer.[58]

Later this right was extended to the accused in criminal cases. In the Court of Chancery the subpoena writ was already developed to force reluctant witnesses to testify. Today most people are both competent and compellable witnesses in the courtroom. But the right to present evidence may on occasion conflict with another rule of evidence such as a privilege shielding information from disclosure. Conflicts of this type have arisen both in this country and in the United States.

In English law there has never been explicit recognition of the existence of a right to present evidence. But case-law seems to suggest that the courts have worked on the assumption that such a right does exist. This can best be illustrated by reference to a series of cases in which the courts have expressed their willingness to override privilege where it is in the interests of a defendant in a criminal trial to do so. In *Marks v Beyfus* (1890) it was said that privilege may be overborne where disclosure is 'necessary or right in order to show the prisoner's innocence'.[59] In *R v Barton* (1972) the defendant, who was a legal executive, was charged with the fraudulent conversion of a legal estate.[60] He served a Crown witness with a notice to produce documents relating to the estate which he claimed established his innocence. The documents had been held to be covered by legal professional privilege. Caulfield J held that they should be produced:

> I cannot conceive that our law would permit a solicitor or other

person to screen from a court information which, if disclosed to a jury, would perhaps enable a man to either establish his innocence or to resist an allegation made by the Crown.[61]

Dicta suggested that the courts were prepared to take a similar approach if a conflict arose between a defendant's request for evidence essential to his case and the public-policy exclusionary rule. In *Conway v Rimmer* (1968)[62] it was noted that the Lord Chancellor had said in a statement to the House of Lords: 'If medical documents or indeed other documents are relevant to the defence in criminal proceedings Crown privilege should not be claimed.'[63] Similarly, where evidence would normally be excluded on the grounds of public policy because it related to police sources of information, Lord Simon indicated that if it was needed by the defence then the usual rules would not apply: 'Sources of police information are a judicially recognised class of evidence unless their production is required to establish innocence in a criminal trial.'[64] More recently, however, there have been indications that the courts may not be willing automatically to allow evidence protected by privilege or the public-policy exclusionary rule to be admitted on the defendant's request. The case which, in the words of T. R. S. Allan,[65] has 'watered down the principle' is *R v Ataou* (1988).[66] A was charged along with two others with conspiracy to supply heroin. Both his co-defendants pleaded guilty, and one of them, H, agreed to testify for the prosecution. Before the trial all three defendants had engaged the same solicitor, but by the time of the hearing H had another solicitor. At the trial A's solicitor passed to A's counsel an attendance note prepared when H had instructed them. This said that H had at that time made a statement in which he said that A had not been involved in heroin dealings. At first instance the judge did not allow H to be cross-examined about this prior inconsistent statement. In the Court of Appeal the conviction of A was set aside. This was not because of the refusal by the judge to remove the privilege but because he had not applied the correct test. There was no automatic rule that privilege should be overridden. It was for the defendant to show that, on the balance of probabilities, the claim of privilege could not be sustained. The judge had to determine whether the legitimate interest of the defendant outweighed that of the party seeking to maintain the privilege.

The courts have now gone on to indicate that that they will use a balancing test to determine whether public-interest immunity would be overridden in a criminal case when evidence is claimed by a defendant to be necessary for him to pursue his case. In *Re Osman (No. 4)*[67] the defendant applied for the writ of habeas corpus. He asked for certain documents to support his claim. When he had sought these documents previously in a separate action he had been refused access to them. The Queen's Bench Divisional Court held that the balancing test to determine disclosure of information subject to public-interest immunity is different in civil and criminal cases. In a criminal case, considerations of the interests of justice in affecting someone's liberty are obviously very great and support disclosure. It is interesting that the courts took pains to stress that cases such as *Marks v Beyfus* were to be regarded as totally separate from the considerations in cases involving public-interest immunity. On the facts of the case they rejected the defendant's claim.

Have the courts in their approach in cases such as *Ataou* and *Osman(No. 4)* strayed too far from the need to safeguard the defendant's interests? T. R. S. Allan suggests that as far as legal professional privilege is concerned the court in *Ataou* indeed went too far. He argues that if a defendant can show that asserting the privilege would impede or weaken his defence, then it should be overridden – with the exception of a situation in which disclosure of the privileged information could be to the detriment of a co-accused. Similar arguments could be advanced that in relation to public-interest immunity the court in *Osman(No. 4)* went too far. Professor J. C. Smith is right to say that: 'If public interest immunity requires the exclusion of evidence which is necessary to prevent a miscarriage of justice, the right course would seem to be to terminate the criminal proceedings.'[68]

The right of a defendant in a criminal trial to present evidence is also included in the European Convention of Human Rights. Article 6 (3) of the Convention provides that:

> Everyone charged with a criminal offence has the following minimum rights . . .
> (d) to examine or have examined witnesses against him and to obtain the attendance and examination of witnesses on his behalf under the same conditions as those against him.

Exclusionary rules of evidence have been challenged under this Article, but not rules of privilege.

In the United States the Constitution provides that the defendant has a right to what is known as 'compulsory process', a constitutional

constitutional right to compel witnesses to testify on his behalf.[69] This right has, on occasion, been used to support a claim by a defendant that the use of a particular evidential privilege was preventing him from putting forward evidence necessary to his case. For example in 1978 a reporter, Myron A. Farber, was jailed when he refused to give evidence in a murder trial.[70] He had raised a state shield law which protected him from testifying. The Supreme Court in New Jersey invalidated the law on the grounds that it was incompatible with the right of the defendant to compulsory process. The courts, though, have not always been prepared to go as far as actually overriding the privilege as such. If the right to present evidence in a criminal trial which has been discussed here is of sufficient strength, then some form of compromise measure both safeguarding the patient's privacy interests and respecting the defendant's rights may be appropriate. When faced with a clash between these rights the courts in America, instead of completely overriding the privilege, have taken one of three possible approaches. In some instances they have dismissed the prosecution completely. For example in cases involving the informer's privilege the court have given the Government the choice of naming the informer or dropping the prosecution completely. Second, on occasion the court have ordered that the testimony of the witness shall be stricken from the record with an admonition to the jury. Alternatively the jury may be allowed to draw an inference that the testimony of the witness if given would have been favourable to the defendant. A. Hill suggests in his article 'Testimonial Privilege' that

> since through discharge or lesser measures detriment to the defendant can be avoided without compelling testimony in derogation of a privilege, such compulsion is inappropriate in the case of privileges created by statute or by state constitution unless as a matter of construction the privilege is deemed inapplicable in the particular circumstances.[71]

To what extent does the defendant's right to obtain evidence in a criminal trial outweigh a privilege protecting doctor–patient confidentiality on the grounds of privacy? It must be emphasised that these rights are not always in conflict. If the medical evidence sought is that of the defendant himself, then, since he wants to produce his own medical information as evidence, the patient should be allowed to waive his privilege. To refuse waiver would be to deny the patient control over access to his own medical evidence in the courtroom. A conflict will arise, however, if the evidence which is sought is that of another person and if that person objects to its production. Essentially the conflict will arise in two types of case:

1 where the defendant wishes to challenge the credibility of a prosecution witness;
2 where he is charged together with another person and they both deny the offence in circumstances in which it is clear that one of them must have committed it, then he may want to call evidence of the co-defendant's propensity to commit the offence.

An example of the former situation is the case of *Toohey v MPC* (1965).[72] The defendant was charged with assault. He wanted to call medical evidence to show that a witness who had testified for the prosecution was suffering from hysteria. It was held in the House of Lords that medical evidence was admissible to show that a witness suffered from a disease, defect or other abnormality of the mind. *Toohey* overruled the decision in *R v Gunewardene* (1951),[73] in which a doctor charged with performing an illegal abortion was prevented from calling medical evidence to the effect that a prosecution witness suffered from a disease which rendered him incapable of telling the truth. An attempt was made in the later decision of *R v Mackeney* (1981)[74] to limit the decision in *Toohey* to where the medical evidence relates to total incapacity to tell the truth, but this has been criticised as being at odds with the judgments in *Toohey* itself.

Whether the defendant should be able to call medical evidence as to the propensity of a co-accused to commit a criminal offence has been the subject of some considerable controversy. It has been suggested that if a defendant shows no sign that he is either insane or suffering from diminished responsibility, then a jury are entitled to form a view concerning his mental state at the time of the alleged offence without requiring expert evidence of his intent. In *Lowery v R* (1974),[75] however, the Privy Council held that evidence of this nature should be admitted. In that case both defendants were at the scene when a girl was murdered. One of them must have committed the crime. Each claimed that the other had committed it. Defendant K sought to adduce psychiatric evidence that L had a personality which made it more likely that he had committed the offence. The Privy Council admitted the evidence. The decision has, however, been the subject of criticism. In the case of *R v Turner* (1975)[76] Lawton LJ held that:

> We adjudge *Lowery v R* to have been decided on its special facts.
> We do not consider that it is authority for the proposition that

in all cases psychologists and psychiatrists can be called to prove the probability of the accused's veracity. If any such rule was applied in our courts trial by psychiatrists would be likely to take the place of trial by jury and magistrates. We do not find that prospect attractive and the law does not provide for it.[77]

The *Turner* approach was later followed in *R v Rimmer and Beech* (1986).[78] The defendants who were jointly charged with murder each claimed in his defence that the other had committed the offence. The judge refused to admit medical evidence to the effect that one of the defendants had a personality that made it more likely that the other had committed the offence on the grounds that such evidence did not go to the main issue in the case.

If a medical-privilege statute had been in existence at the time that the above cases were heard, then it is certainly possible that debarring access to the medical information would have produced a different result. Does this mean that any privilege should specifically provide that it would not be applicable if the innocence of the defendant was in dispute, or would a better alternative be the use of some sort of compromise measure such as has been adopted elsewhere? Should, for example, the prosecution be dropped if objection was raised to the production of medical evidence? Is this really desirable or practicable if the prosecution in question involves a very grave crime?

Alternatively the court could draw some form of inference in favour of the defendant who wants the evidence to be adduced. But this may be unjust. Consider the implications of drawing such an inference in the light of one Canadian case.[79] A husband and wife were charged with assault upon their child. They each denied the charge. The husband sought to adduce evidence that the wife had been receiving psychotherapy. If the evidence is excluded totally, this could lead to an unjust verdict, for the evidence might be very relevant. If the court allows the medical evidence to remain confidential but allows adverse inferences to be drawn, this may also be highly unjust to the mother. The psychiatric records may be inconclusive. If the mother has, for example, told the psychiatrist that she often felt like hitting her child, what does this establish? Many mothers undergoing psychotherapy may express the same feeling, but it does not necessarily mean that they have assaulted the child. The mother may not be objecting to the evidence being given of the consultation with the psychiatrist because it is incriminating but because it is embarrassing. In such a case if an inference were to be drawn, it could lead to a wrong conviction.

The drawback with these compromise solutions is that at some point we are forced to choose between the two rights which have been identified. If a defendant in a criminal case claims that disclosure of confidential medical information should be made because it is necessary for his defence, then the patient's right to privacy should take second place to the right to present evidence. But this exception should not be absolute; a privilege statute should provide a safeguard against it being overridden automatically. A threshold test should be introduced. I return to this issue in chapter 5.

Other interests

The right to privacy as it is enacted in the European Convention of Human Rights provides that it may be restricted if such limitations are necessary for the prevention of crime and disorder and the preservation of health and public morals. These are interests of what can be termed a 'public' nature. The rules of evidence in this country and elsewhere have been limited by courts and legislatures on similar 'public' grounds.

As far as those privileges which exist in English law at present are concerned, the courts have held that where the privilege is being used as a means of concealing evidence of crime or fraud the privilege will be overridden. In *R v Cox and Railton* (1884)[80] the defendant consulted a solicitor for the purpose of drawing up a bill of sale which later proved to be fraudulent. The court held that if the reason why the defendant had consulted a solicitor was that of committing a crime or fraud, then the consultation was not privileged. Stephen J held that such an exception was necessary because otherwise a person intending to commit treason or murder could seek legal advice for the purpose of doing so with impunity.

The court has applied the same principles in civil actions. In *Williams v Quebrad Railway Land and Copper Co Ltd* (1895)[81] Kekewich J held that while it is of vital importance that the rule of privilege protection should not be departed from, at the same time

> where there is anything of an underhand nature or
> approaching to fraud especially in commercial matters
> where there should be the veriest good faith the whole
> transaction should be ripped out and disclosed in all
> its nakedness to the light of the court.[82]

He went on to hold that this limitation applied even where a solicitor to the party charged with fraud is not himself charged with being a party to the fraud.

It can be argued that there are analogous considerations of public policy which apply when we consider the scope of a medical professional privilege. Medical evidence may be crucial in a criminal case. The existence of a medical professional privilege could lead to the dismissal of the prosecution if the privilege is not waived. In a murder trial medical evidence may be needed to show how the victim died and to establish that the cause of the death was the actions of the defendant rather than those of another person. A good illustration of the importance of medical evidence is provided by the English case of *R v Blaue* (1975).[83] The facts in this case concerned a Jehovah's Witness who was stabbed. She was taken to hospital, where she refused a blood transfusion because of her religious beliefs. This transfusion would have saved her life. Her assailant was charged with murder, but was convicted of manslaughter on the grounds of diminished responsibility. If a medical professional privilege statute had existed, then this could have presented grave problems. Though evidence could have been given of the fact that the witness had died, no evidence concerning the cause of death or the course of the medical treatment, including her refusal to have a blood transfusion, could have been given by those involved in the treatment unless it could be shown that the victim had waived the privilege. The medical profession bind themselves to preserve, after the death of the patient, confidentiality of that patient's communications. An example of the importance of medical evidence as circumstantial evidence in a criminal case is shown in the case of *R v Apicella* (1985).[84] In this case the defendant was charged with three counts of rape. Each of the alleged victims had developed an unusual strain of gonorrhoea. While in prison the defendant had been seen by a consultant for therapeutic reasons. He was tested for gonorrhoea, the consultant assuming that he was consenting when in fact he was not. The test revealed that the defendant was suffering from the same type of gonorrhoea. If a medical privilege statute had been in existence when that case had been decided, this would have resulted in the evidence being excluded, which could have had the consequence that a guilty man went free.

In the United States medical professional privilege has been held to apply to both civil and criminal cases except where the legislature has limited the medical-privilege statute to civil cases[85] or where the courts have held that the privilege is to be interpreted as being inapplicable in criminal cases. In Idaho in the case of *State v Bounds* (1953)[86] the defendant was charged with driving under the influence of intoxicating liquor and while so driving colliding with another car. The prosecution cross-examined the doctor concerning the statements made by the defendant soon afterwards. The court held that this evidence had been correctly admitted and that the statutory privilege did not apply to criminal cases. In *People v Lane* in California (1893),[87] another prosecution for murder, it was held that a statutory privilege was not conferred to shield those charged with murder. While not removing privilege protection totally in criminal cases, some jurisdictions have limited its application in criminal litigation, holding, for example, that it does not apply in those criminal cases in which the defendant is charged with causing the death of or inflicting serious injuries upon other individuals.

Other cases in which it could be said that the public-policy considerations override evidential privilege are those concerning the custody and care of children. Exclusion of medical evidence could leave the court unaware that a parent may have a medical condition which makes him unfit to have the custody of his children. Take a situation in which a husband believes that a wife is unfit to have the custody of their children. In support of his claim he may want to show that his wife is prone to hard drinking and depressive phases, for which she has been seeking psychiatric treatment. The wife may oppose her condition being brought into issue. In such cases most of the evidence is in the form of a report which is compiled by the court welfare officer. Concerning the contents of this report,

> Although there are no formal guidelines regarding how a court welfare officer should prepare his report it is expected that he will visit and interview various persons including the child at their respective homes and if necessary to extend inquiries to the wider family, school, family doctor and other persons whose observations may be helpful.[88]

Were a privilege statute to be in operation, it is likely that the wife would claim that the doctor was not entitled to give that information to the court welfare officer and would attempt to stop it from being disclosed in the courtroom. This could, however, have the consequence that a child was put at risk of harm from an unfit parent if the wife were to be given custody.

In the United States the courts have been prepared in a number of cases to hold that a physician–patient privilege statute did not apply to cases concerning the custody of children. In *People v Chitty* (1963),[89] the court rejected a claim of privilege concerning the medical and hospital records of the child's father, holding that the rights of the father were secondary to those of the child. A similar approach was taken in *D v D* (1969).[90] In this case the court held that a wife could claim privilege for medical records involving treatment in a psychiatric hospital from discovery by her husband. None the less the court did have an interest in making a correct and proper determination of the suitability of the person who was to be granted care and custody of a child, and therefore the court were able to subpoena the records *in camera* for inspection by the court. In another jurisdiction, however, the courts did hold that privilege did bar access to medical records. In *Koshman v Superior Court of Sacramento County* (1980),[91] a Californian court held that records which concerned the hospitalisation of the mother for an alleged overdose of narcotics were not available for discovery by the father in his action to obtain custody of their two children, since the mother had asserted her physician-patient privilege. The father's argument that the mother had waived her privilege by putting her medical condition into issue in attempt to obtain custody was rejected. The court in this case suggested that the state legislature might contemplate modifying the statutory privilege so that it could be overridden in order to determine where the best interests of the child might lie.

The public interest in protecting the welfare of children is shown also in those court decisions and statutory provisions which limit the applicability of medical professional privilege in cases involving child abuse. The need to ensure that the interests of children are protected has already led to reform in the law of evidence in England and Wales. Provision has been made to enable children's evidence to be given through live television links.[92] The Children's Act 1989 provides in section 98 (1) that in care proceedings and emergency protection orders, the general rule that a witness may refuse to answer a question which has the effect of incriminating him does not apply.[93] However, it is noticeable that discussion of exceptions to legal professional privilege or to public-policy rules has rarely included any reference to the need to safeguard the interests of a child and to override privilege on that account. In the case of *Re D* (1970),[94] in which the application by a mother for disclosure of the local authority's case records was rejected, Lord Denning appeared to suggest that there could be exceptional circumstances in which a court might override legal professional privilege. But his words were not part of the decision in that case, which concerned public-interest immunity. The tragedies which have resulted through unwise decisions being made concerning the safety of children outside the courtroom should not be mirrored by a legislative enactment which prevents the court from discovering that the patient is unsuitable for the care and control of his child or inhibiting the prosecution in a case of child abuse.

The law should, it is submitted, recognise that there are weighty public interests which may qualify the rights-based privilege justification suggested above. Although I do not believe that the simple fact that the case before the court is a criminal prosecution is by itself an automatic justification for privilege being overridden, nevertheless there are certain criminal cases in which the public interest in obtaining access to all relevant evidence is particularly strong. This is the case when the proceedings involve grave crimes. There is also a clear public interest in ensuring that the welfare of children is safeguarded, and in such cases the privacy interest of the patient should be overborne. Defining the precise ambit of these exceptions is an issue to which I will return later.

POSSIBLE OBJECTIONS

Having declared my preferred alternative rooted in the right to privacy, I shall endeavour to anticipate some of the criticisms which may be levelled at my conclusions. In discussing the problems of implementing a rule of evidence which would exclude evidence which has been obtained illegally or improperly Dennis comments that it is difficult to talk in terms of rights and then to try to limit them pragmatically.[95]

> The difficulty with such balancing-type suggestions is that once we concede that 'rights' can be traded against social goals such as the preservation of reliable evidence we lose the notion of a right in its proper sense. As Dworkin has argued, to take rights seriously is to regard them as trumps. They prevail over utilitarian goals.[96]

That type of objection is one which I am open to here. If I believe so strongly in rights, then why do I have to qualify them? While you might not like the fact that a privilege excludes evidence in serious criminal cases, is that not the price you have to pay? I concede the philosophical inconsistency in my argument and that moreover by 'watering down' rights I may be seen as weakening them. But while rights are important, I believe that in practice they have to be balanced against other considerations. Rather than present an analysis which is perhaps philosophically consistent but ignores the practical realities of the way in which the legal system operates, I have endeavoured to look at other considerations which are, I suggest, of importance. Ethical analysis assists us to identify questions of concern. But philosophy provides us with the tools for reasoning and not with the answers to the questions of practical importance which assail us. It is for us to make the choice.

Others may criticise me on the grounds that I place too much stress upon the whole idea of rights altogether. The Younger Committee considered that the right to privacy was something too uncertain to be enforced in English law.[97] I would argue that the notion of privacy may be conceptually difficult to grasp but that that does not mean that it should be ignored. Regardless even of the legal recognition of the right to privacy, we surely have some obligation to grant respect to the autonomy of the individual. Respect for the individual's right to foster meaningful relationships under the aegis of confidentiality is surely part of this. While in theory at least the balance of rights may be in favour of protecting medical confidential information in the courtroom, there is still, perhaps, a (slight) question mark over the strength of that justification. Is medical confidentiality really an absolute enduring obligation, or something much weaker? In the next chapter I consider whether confidentiality in medical practice today is little more than rhetoric.

4

CONFIDENTIALITY: RHETORIC OR REALITY?

The doctor–patient relationship has long been regarded as the epitome of the relationship of trust and confidence. The patient places trust in his medical practitioner and relies on that practitioner to respect that trust. The medical profession have traditionally pledged themselves to uphold such an ethic. The Hippocratic oath, for example, provided: 'Whatever in connection with my professional practice I see or hear in the life of men which ought not to be spoken of abroad I shall not divulge reckoning that all such should remain secret.' But just how real is this obligation in modern-day medical practice? Today the medical profession accord homage at a rhetorical level to the general principle of confidentiality, yet at the same time they regard a list of exceptions to the principle as ethically justifiable. These exceptions are incorporated in the ethical codes of both the General Medical Council and the British Medical Association.[1] In addition, modern methods of medical practice force us to view the ethic from a different perspective. Today a patient is just as likely to receive treatment in a large impersonal institution as in the relatively cosy surroundings of a GP's surgery. Perceptions of what information is 'confidential' may also vary. Someone who has a broken leg, for example, will not be expected to say that it is an ailment which is confidential in the same sense as a venereal disease contracted by another patient.

But if confidentiality is on closer examination a value more honoured in the breach than the observance, why should we bother to uphold it at all? Why enact an evidential privilege if doctor–patient communications in practice are not treated as confidential outside the courtroom? Even if confidentiality is generally observed but is in practice safeguarded more rigorously in some areas than others, this may suggest to us that this variable approach to confidentiality should

71

be reflected in the operation of any privilege that is enacted. But which areas of medical practice have that special quality of confidence?

This chapter examines exactly where the boundaries of confidentiality in medical practice lie today. First, the classical notions of confidentiality and the extent to which they have survived in modern medical practice are discussed. Second, I examine just how wide are the exceptions to confidentiality contained within the medical profession's ethical code. Finally, I ask whether unauthorised disclosure of patient information makes talk of patient confidentiality in practice wholly unrealistic.

CONFIDENTIALITY: THE BASIC POSITION

The medical practitioner is bound by his ethical code to keep silent regarding those things which are communicated to him by his patient. Phillips and Dawson have put forward two justifications for this requirement.[2] First, the doctor's silence is a necessary part of the patient's right to privacy. If the doctor discloses the information about him to a third party without his consent, then the patient has been denied the right to control access to his own personal information. Second, if the patient is aware that a doctor is likely to disclose information about him, whether during his lifetime or after his death, to third parties, then he may be discouraged from coming forward for treatment. This is particularly the case if the medical information is of extreme social sensitivity. Consider the devastating personal consequences if the fact that a person has contracted HIV is disclosed in this way.

This ethical obligation continues during the lifetime of the patient and after his death. Because the obligation forms part of the ethical code of the medical profession, if the doctor breaks confidence he may find that he is liable to be disciplined by his professional body, the General Medical Council. At the very least he will find that he meets considerable censure from his fellow health professionals. The two cases which follow are celebrated examples of situations in which doctors who published details of patient medical information without the patient's consent after the patient's death found themselves the subject of powerful criticism.

After Sir Winston Churchill died, his physician Lord Moran wrote a book entitled *Churchill: The Struggle for Survival (1944-1965)*.[3] The book chronicled the latter years of Churchill's premiership, when he suffered a severe decline in health. Publication of the book led to much controversy and critical comment from fellow members of the medical profession. Similarly in 1983 the *British Medical Journal* published an obituary of Gladwin Buttle.[4] He was at the forefront of the development of blood transfusions on a large scale during the Second World War. The obituary mentioned that he had treated a General Wingate after the General had cut his own throat. Many at the time were of the opinion that Wingate was insane. But Buttle said that the General's blood was swimming with malarial parasites. This revelation was recounted in the obituary. The editor of the *British Medical Journal* received a letter from the General Medical Council which informed him that although the details in the obituary were by no means disparaging towards the General, the disclosure was nevertheless in breach of confidence.

The Wingate example illustrates that the obligation of confidentiality extends beyond what have been referred to by the American jurist Wigmore as 'active' confidences – those transmitted by word of mouth – to 'passive confidences' (the doctor's observance of the physical and mental condition of the patient) and to information which has been gained from tests.[5]

To what extent has medical confidentiality survived in modern medical practice? This traditional notion of medical confidentiality works best in the scenario of the one-to-one doctor–patient relationship. While this approach is still to be found in certain areas of practice, in many others the patient is cared for by a group of health professionals. I begin by looking at what may be at present the doctor–patient relationship closest to that of the traditional model, that of psychiatrist–patient.

MEDICAL PRACTICE AND DILEMMAS OF CONFIDENTIALITY

The psychotherapist/psychiatrist–patient relationship

Confidentiality is regarded as crucial by those involved in the care of mentally ill or emotionally disturbed patients. A stigma has traditionally surrounded those with mental disorders. People may no longer go for an afternoon's entertainment to watch the lunatics incarcerated in Bedlam (as the Bethlehem Royal Hospital was popularly known), but there remains considerable fear and mistrust of mental illness and those who suffer from it. Miles has suggested that the reason for this is that mental illness is regarded by society as a stigma.

> It is popularly thought of as a serious condition with little chance of full recovery which hits people of not very admirable character. Moreover the trouble is located in the 'mind' of the sick person and people tend to think that thereby the most essential part of the human being becomes questionable or discreditable. As Goffman pertinently phrased it, the stigmatised is regarded as less than human.[6]

Preservation of confidentiality is necessary to ensure that patients are prepared to come forward for treatment and that they continue with treatment. Patients require that assurance. They do not want the risk of becoming the butt of cruel jokes and being socially ostracised.

A patient may visit a psychiatrist or a psychotherapist for treatment of his mental illness. While there is some overlap between psychiatry and psychotherapy in that practitioners of psychiatry may engage in psychotherapy, there are differences between the two forms of patient care. The psychiatrist will usually be involved with patients who suffer from an illness such as schizophrenia or severe depression. He relies usually upon conventional methods of treatment such as the use of drugs. In contrast the psychotherapist deals with those patients who suffer from, for example, chronic neurosis, anxiety and personality disorders. The psychotherapist will often employ very different methods from those used by the psychiatrist. For example psychotherapists use psychoanalysis, elucidating the root of the individual's problem over a long period of time by means of discussion. This may take the form of a one-to-one encounter or may take place during a group therapy session in which individual problems are examined by members of the group with the aid of a therapist who acts as group leader. A long period of therapy will leave the therapist in possession of a considerable amount of very sensitive personal information. 'The psychiatric patient confides more utterly than any one else in the world. He exposes to the therapist not only what his words directly express; he lays bare his entire self, his dreams, his fantasies, his sins and shames.'[7] Practitioners in this area stress the fact that they take great pains to preserve their patients' confidentiality. Medical records contain only the briefest of details, aiming to ensure that there is no unauthorised access to the records.

But though the patient consulting a psychiatrist may rest safe in the knowledge that the practitioner is bound by the medical profession's ethical code to preserve confidentiality since he is simply a registered medical practitioner who has chosen to specialise in psychiatry, the situation is more complex regarding psychotherapists. Unlike medical practitioners, as we shall see later, there is no central system of registration for psychotherapists. As a result it is possible for anyone to practise psychotherapy, and a wide variety of persons presently do so, including medical practitioners, other health workers and even teachers. Without a central system of professional organisation the patient may well feel uneasy about the confidentiality of his personal information. There has been a movement in recent years among psychotherapists to organise themselves and to mark out their professional status.[8] The Sieghart Report in 1976 recommended that there should be statutory regulation of psychotherapists, with a Council for Psychotherapy being set up and training courses being established. After a series of Rugby Conferences – the name derived from the location of the first such conference – the United Kingdom Standing Conference for Psychotherapy was formed. Its Constitution states that it aims 'To promote or assist in the promotion of the preservation of public health by encouraging high standards of training and practice in psychotherapy'.[9] At present the Conference is some way off establishing psychotherapy as an independent profession, and as yet it lacks a defined code of ethics. This lack of an ethical code makes the protection of confidentiality even less certain than in the conventional medical practitioner–patient relationship.

Despite the emphasis upon the need to keep confidence in psychiatric medicine, even here the value is still not absolute. The ethical code of the medical profession, which applies to psychiatrists and to those psychotherapists who are registered medical practitioners, admits of many exceptions, as we shall see later. The patient receiving treatment or psychotherapeutic counselling for mental illness or psychiatric problems may find that personal information could be divulged by his medical practitioner if the practitioner decides that it falls under one of the exceptions contained in that ethical code. For example if the patient is suffering from schizophrenia but is attempting to lead a normal life in the community, then it is regarded as very important that both his family and the social services should be aware of this in order that they can provide support. A psychiatrist may also feel constrained to break confidentiality when the patient may cause harm to another. This dilemma too is considered in detail later.

The general practitioner–patient relationship

The general practitioner is the medical professional with whom a patient is most likely to come into contact. He is responsible for long-term continuing personal care. At first sight this appears to be the classical doctor–patient relationship of confidence and trust. On closer examination, however, the relationship is shown to be far less straightforward. The level of confidentiality here may depend upon the nature of the ailment – whether, for example, the patient complains of a sprained ankle or fears that he has contracted venereal disease. This problem is exacerbated in that not all patients may regard the same condition as having the same level of confidentiality. A gynaecological problem may be something which a young girl has great difficulty in discussing with her medical practitioner, and she may be adamant that no one else should know about it. An older woman may feel no such inhibition. The level of sensitivity between different ailments may also vary between those of different cultural and ethnic groups.

It is a feature of everyday medical practice that now patients are very rarely treated by one medical practitioner during the whole of their lives. Care of the patient is usually undertaken by a team of doctors, nurses, social workers and others such as home helps. The most simple form of the 'team' arrangement is that of the group practice.[10] In such a practice several doctors are based in the same building and the patient, once he is registered with one of the doctors, can go to any of the other practitioners for treatment. His medical records will be seen by any of the doctors whom he consults. It is questionable to what extent the passage of such information can really be regarded as a breach of confidence. It can be argued that if a patient goes for treatment to a doctor other than the one with whom he is registered, he is impliedly consenting to the doctor having access to details of his previous medical treatment. Further, the other doctors who acquire information about the patient for the purposes of medical treatment are themselves bound by the same obligation of confidentiality as the first doctor in that practice who treats that patient. A more difficult situation may arise if persons other than medical practitioners are involved in the treatment of the patient. This can occur both in the context of the group practice and also in that of a relatively new phenomenon, the community practice. In group practices the patient is commonly given the option of seeing a nurse as opposed to a doctor. As will be seen below, nurses are also bound by professional obligations of confidentiality.[11] This prompts the question, if we are entitled to assume that in such a situation the patient has impliedly consented to the breach of confidentiality, should we include the nurse within the ambit of privilege protection?

Somewhat different questions face us in the context of a 'community practice'. In such a practice the doctor works alongside other health-care professionals in a 'total care' process. The emphasis in such a practice is upon the welfare of the individual patient in the context of both his needs and those of the community at large. A doctor who works in a community practice may find himself faced with a dilemma of whether or not to pass on the information regarding patients to colleagues in the practice. The approach of the doctor to health care is rooted in the notion of resolving the medical problems of the individual patient. In contrast, fellow professionals working in the same practice may have different priorities. The social worker who is often a member of such a practice has a role which has been defined as that of

> the purposeful and ethical application of personal skills in an interpersonal relationship directed towards enhancing the personal and social functioning of an individual, family, group, neighbourhood which necessarily involves using evidence obtained from practice in order to create a social environment conducive to all.[12]

This is not to say that in all situations the aim of doctors and social workers will diverge. Huw W. S. Francis gives an example of a family doctor who sees a lady with arthritis. He decides that the lady needs social support as well as medical treatment.[13] With the consent of the patient he discusses her case with a social worker. Both the doctor and the social worker have a similar ethic, that of loyalty to the patient, and they are working together for the recovery of the patient. But, there is the danger that although a patient may have consented to information being passed to the social worker in order that the social worker can assist the patient with her problems, the social worker may decide to use the information for a wider purpose such as alleviating the problems of the family as a whole. Though Francis mentions that the doctor and the social worker have a similar ethic, it is not an identical one. A doctor who works in a community practice may be placed in a difficult dilemma. If he declines to pass on information to the social worker, he may frustrate the aim behind the practice. Instead of working as an integrated team the practice could fragment, with some members working towards the aim of caring for the community at large while others are concentrating their attention upon individual members to the exclusion of the wider community. Alternatively, if he does decide to pass on sensitive personal information, that could lead to a considerable infringement of the patient's confidentiality. The British Medical Association have drafted their guidelines in such a way that the onus as to which approach to take is placed on the individual doctor. They suggest that confidentiality places little real difficulty in the working relationship between doctors and social workers as long as personal confidentiality between the professions is preserved. But they then go on to note that since the British Association of Social Workers' ethical code does not have sanctions such as those which may be imposed by the General Medical Council, the doctor must bear in mind that it is he who has the responsibility for any disclosure that he makes.

It was mentioned above that there is uncertainty over whether the information passed between doctor and patient is inherently confidential, where the doctor in question was a general practitioner. This uncertainty has led to the development of what is known as 'negotiated confidentiality'. Doctor and patient agree on the boundaries of confidentiality of information disclosed by the patient, and in what circumstances disclosure can take place. The principal advocates of this approach are Ian Thompson and Paul Sieghart.[14] Such a concept of negotiated confidentiality has been adapted from use in social work, where it has been the practice for several years for professional and client to negotiate what is and what is not confidential. Thompson suggests that experience in social work has shown that very little is truly confidential, but that which is confidential should remain so. In his view the interests of patients and of doctors would best be resolved by open and explicit discussion as to where the boundaries of confidentiality should lie. It is interesting to note that Thompson in advocating this also supports the idea of an evidential privilege. Negotiated confidentiality may not be consistent with a traditional evidential privilege. While being praiseworthy in promoting candour between doctor and patient, it leads us to ask, why keep completely silent about all doctor–patient confidences in the courtroom when the medical profession themselves have not agreed to absolute confidentiality outside the courtroom? There are also practical problems with negotiated confidentiality. Margaret Brazier makes the point that it is difficult for doctors and patients to predict those circumstances which may call for a breach of an obligation not to disclose.[15] But, if it is possible to identify and to treat separately those elements in a doctor–patient relationship which the parties have agreed should be treated as 'confidential', then those elements must have a strong claim to be kept confidential in court.

Confidentiality and hospital care

The classical approach to medical confidentiality of a one-to-one doctor–patient relationship where the patient discloses confidences to his doctor which his doctor binds himself not to divulge is almost unrecognisable in the context of hospital care.

In practice a person who enters hospital will frequently be unaware of the extent to which he will be examined and treated by junior doctors, anaesthetists and surgeons. A large number of these medical personnel will also have access to the patient's records. Just how large a number came as a surprise to one American consultant, Siegler, when he was forced to carry out a survey after one of his patients threatened to leave hospital unless he was told how many people did have access to his medical records. Siegler was staggered to discover that at least seventy-five and possibly as many as a hundred medical personnel had legitimate access to that patient's records. This number would probably have been higher had the patient's treatment been more complex or had he been treated in a teaching hospital.[16]

Does this mean that there is no respect for the value of confidentiality in hospitals? Surely not. Those medical personnel who are involved in the treatment of hospital patients are themselves bound by obligations of confidence, whether these are contained in declarations of ethics or in their contracts. Nurses, for example, are bound by their professional code to preserve patients' confidences.[17]

The *Code of Professional Conduct for the Nurse, Midwife and Health Visitor*, published by the United Kingdom Central Council for Nursing, Midwifery and Health Visitors, provides in clause 9 that:

> Each registered nurse, midwife and health visitor is accountable for his or her practice and, in the exercise of professional accountability, shall:
>
> 9. Respect confidential information obtained in the course of professional practice and refrain from disclosing such information without the consent of the patient/client or a person entitled to act on his/her behalf, except where disclosure is

required by law or by order of the court or is necessary in the public interest.[18]

The transfer of information between different health-care professionals can be likened to the transfer of information between doctors in a group practice in that it is essential for the care of the individual patient. Perhaps it can be argued that by entering hospital the patient implicitly waives a certain proportion of his confidentiality if the free passage of his personal information is necessary for his care.

But, just as in the area of general practice the doctor can be faced with a difficult decision if those he works alongside have different ethical codes, this situation may arise in the hospital situation. Dora Black and Fiona Subotsky give an example of the conflicts which may arise in the area of child psychiatry.[19] The child psychiatrist may well be involved with social workers in caring for the child. This may create problems, since social workers are, unlike other health professionals, not compelled to register with a disciplinary body but are responsible to the social services department of their local authority. Moreover in some areas they are required to give identifiable information regarding clients which is then put on computer for storage.

It is important to note that the exact level of confidentiality given to patient information may vary dramatically between areas of medical practice. While in some hospitals patients' records are literally left lying around, in others, for example those hospitals engaged in the treatment of AIDS patients, the staff take stringent precautions to preserve the maximum amount of security possible.[20] A further problem concerning confidentiality in the area of hospital medicine is that the decision as to whether to release patient medical information to third parties is not in the hands of the doctors who have been treating the patient but in the hands of hospital administrators. Although the doctor may himself pledge to keep the patient's confidences, this assurance can in practice be overridden.

Some special problems

In addition to the main types of medical practice which I have considered so far there are many medical practitioners who are employed outside the National Health Service by large commercial agencies to provide health care for members of that agency. Examples of such medical practitioners are the occupational health physician, the prison medical officer and the army surgeon. All these medical practitioners suffer from special constraints upon their role. While, as registered medical practitioners, they are subject to the ethical constraints of the General Medical Council, they are also under obligations to their employers. This dual loyalty may lead to particular problems.

The occupational health physician is appointed by a firm to oversee the health of the firm's employees.[21] Not all firms possess their own occupational health physician: this may depend upon factors such as the size of the firm and the financial resources which the firm is able or prepared to devote to health care. Some firms use the occupational health services provided by commercial organisations. The occupational health doctor is in no way a substitute for the employee's own medical practitioner. Although individual employees may receive treatment from him if an accident occurs at the workplace, this usually takes the form of the first line of treatment before the patient is referred elsewhere. The physician performs many roles which differ from those of the doctor in private practice. The occupational health physician may have a far greater educational role than his counterpart in private practice. An important part of the occupational physician's work is the assessments he makes in order to determine if an employee is fit for work after a long absence.

While it has been stressed that an occupational health physician is subject to the same ethical obligation of confidentiality as he would be were he a general practitioner, concern has been expressed about how far this obligation is adhered to in the work setting. In practice most employees consent to disclosure of their medical information. For example a medical report is often stipulated as a condition of employment. But, if the employee requires that confidence should be kept, then the doctor is bound to comply. Diana Kloss notes the importance of keeping the obligation:

> This means that if the employee moves to a different employment he should be asked to give written consent to the transfer of medical records to his new employer. The need for care in such matters is illustrated by one case where an occupational health physician routinely notified an employee's GP of the employee's raised blood pressure. Later the man failed to obtain life insurance because the insurance company insisted on a medical report from his GP.[22]

Some firms clearly recognise the doctor's obligation of confidentiality in their codes of practice. For example the United Biscuits handbook provides that:

> The company's health care specialists are employed as impartial and their actions are governed at all times by their professional code of ethics. Access to clinical data is confined to OH (Occupational Health) physicians and nurses and no confidential information may be disclosed to others without the consent of the employee.[23]

The occupational health physician does, however, also have a duty to his employer to safeguard the health of his employees, and on occasion he may feel that he must break confidence in order to avoid harm being caused to other employees of the firm. This breach of confidence may be justified under the exception to the general duty of confidence contained in the General Medical Council's ethical code relating to the interests of society in general. This exception should not, however, be invoked lightly. The problem with the occupational health physician, as with any employed medical practitioner, is that he may form an unduly cosy relationship with his employers. One commentator writing in a letter to the *Journal of Medical Ethics* has commented in relation to the decision to break confidence that: 'Too often such decisions reflect not the moral codes of the medical profession but rather the personality of the doctor who desires so to please that he forgets his ethical moral obligations.'[24] Even more acute problems of confidentiality will arise in the case of the prison medical officer. Unlike the occupational health physician he is in effect the sole source of medical care available to the prisoner. Paul Bowden has commented that the prison medical officer has what is in effect a tri-partite role within the prison structure.[25] He is, first, a doctor caring for his patient, the prisoner, and he owes that prisoner his professional ethical obligation. Second, he has a role in supporting the institution of the prison by, for example, advising upon what type of penal establishment the prisoner is best suited for both physically and mentally. Third, there are activities which in Bowden's words 'support the state'. These include, for example, informing the governor of information of which the prison medical officer may become aware as a result of a medical examination of the patient and which may assist in identifying the patient. While, therefore, he owes an obligation of confidence, this must inevitably be tempered by the institutional constraints within which he operates. This is shown byhis role in the operation of the Viral Infectivity Restrictions.[26] Originally developed as a means of tackling the problem of hepatitis B, they are now being used as a method of dealing with AIDS in the prison system. If a prisoner tests HIV positive, then 'VIR' is written in his file. The medical officer may also make other orders in relation to the work and recreational activity which such a prisoner may undertake. It appears that the restrictions have been operated in such a way that the majority of these prisoners are being segregated. At present, if a prisoner tests HIV positive this fact becomes generally known. This does not mean that the obligation of confidentiality in the prison system has been totally abandoned but that in certain areas it is less than absolute. The Woolf Enquiry into the disturbances in English prisons during 1990 in their broad recommendations relating to the prison system commented that 'HIV positive prisoners must not and need not become the pariahs of the prison system.'[27] They criticised the operation of Viral Infectivity Restrictions. They commented favourably upon the Scottish experience. In Saughton Prison in Edinburgh an important part of the innovative multi-disciplinary approach to dealing with prisoners with HIV has involved a strong policy which emphasises confidentiality.[28]

It appears, then, from the above study of different areas of medical practice that the obligation of confidence is far less clear-cut than might at first glance appear. The position is further complicated when we examine the exceptions to the general obligation of confidence recognised in the medical profession's code of ethics.

AUTHORISED EXCEPTIONS

The General Medical Council provide a list of eight specified circumstances in which a doctor may properly breach confidentiality:

1 where the patient or his legal advisor gives consent;
2 where information is shared with other doctors, nurses and health-care professionals caring for the patient;
3 where, on medical grounds, it is undesirable to seek the patient's consent, information regarding the patient's health may be given to a close relative;
4 when, in the opinion of the doctor, disclosure of information to someone other than a relative would be in the best interests of the patient, the doctor must make every effort to get the patient's

consent, but if this is not obtained and he believes that disclosure is in the patient's best interests, then he may go ahead and disclose;

5 where information is required to be disclosed in pursuance of a specific statutory requirement;

6 information may be disclosed where disclosure is ordered by a court;

7 disclosure may be made in the public interest;

8 information may be disclosed if it is necessary for the purposes of a medical research project approved by a recognised ethical committee.

Written consent, information shared with other health-care professionals caring for the patient

While the BMA in their *Handbook* provide that the general obligation of confidentiality may be overridden if the patient gives his consent, the GMC are more circumspect: they provide that written consent is needed. If true consent is granted, respect will have been given to the patient's right to control access to his own personal information.

But what amounts to 'true consent' for these purposes? Mason and McCall Smith suggest that in practice the patient may be under a certain amount of pressure to agree to his medical information being disclosed.[29] In a teaching hospital there is what they regard as almost overwhelming pressure upon the patient to agree to a junior doctor being present at a consultation. It could be argued, however, that when a patient enters a teaching hospital, he is aware of the risks of this happening. At least one major hospital in the North of England which has a continual flow of medical students through its wards indicates on its appointment cards that students may be present when patients are receiving treatment. There is also the problem that even if the patient's consent is not coerced, it may still not be fully informed consent. In 1977 and again in 1978 BBC2 broadcast eight television programmes in the series *Hospital*. These amounted to an in-depth examination of Bolton Area Health Authority. They used a 'fly-on-the-wall' technique which had been used in other documentaries. The programmes went into considerable detail and showed patients in various stages of treatment. Death, incontinence and nakedness were frankly portrayed. The BBC employed a nurse to obtain the consent of patients to the broadcasts. But it has been questioned just how real those consents were. Huw W. S. Francis noted that few of the patients were able to see the programmes before they were broadcast.[30] Moreover, the form that the patient signed fell far short of the medical requirement of full consent.

The GMC provide in their ethical code that confidentiality may be broken if the information is passed to other health-care professionals caring for the patient. Thus, the general practitioner who passes on medical records in a group practice is covered by this exception, as is the hospital where the patient receives care from a co-ordinated team of doctors and nurses. While most individuals who undergo medical treatment impliedly consent to a certain amount of access by other medical practitioners to their medical records, situations may arise in which, while the doctor may believe that the information needs to be transmitted to facilitate patient care, the patient himself does not want confidentiality to be broken. Breaking confidence against the patient's express wishes would lead to the patient's right to privacy being infringed. This form of breach of confidence has been particularly criticised in the context of the patient with AIDS. Rannan Gillon, when writing about complaints made by medical practitioners that consultants in sexually transmitted disease clinics had been unwilling to pass on to them details regarding AIDS sufferers, argued that it is wrong to override confidentiality because the doctor automatically assumes that it is in the patient's interests to facilitate his health care[31] 'A vital aspect of doing good for one's patients is to discount your own perception of what is good for them in favour of their own autonomous beliefs.'[32] In the case of a patient with an illness of such social sensitivity as AIDS the mere fact that another person was involved in the patient's care was not an automatic justification for that patient's medical information being transferred to him. Moreover, it is unlikely that care of the patient will be neglected by that medical information not being transferred, since the patient will be under the care of the consultant in the clinic.

Disclosure to third parties in the interests of the patient

The GMC divide this category into two parts. The first is that disclosure may be justified to a close relative if, on medical grounds, it is undesirable to obtain the patient's consent. The second is that in exceptional circumstances disclosure may be made to a third party who is not a close relative in the interests of the patient. Some authors do not appear to be unduly worried by the existence of this exception. Mason and McCall Smith, for example, argue that such instances of breach of confidence are rare, and in any case, since they are a matter for clinical judgment, they should not be questioned.[33]

But is that satisfactory? Is confidentiality simply a concept developed to facilitate thorough and effective clinical practice, or is it a method of protecting the rights of the individual patient? This exception has been criticised. Margaret Brazier has maintained that if a patient expressly places a ban upon communication with a third party then the doctor must respect it: 'The patient is entitled to confidentiality and is entitled to require that it be maintained even where contrary to his interests.'[34]

Similarly Kottow argues that the exception is paternalistic and that rationally competent individuals are allowed to take decisions which may act against their own interests, and doing so does not make them irrational. If we take the view that entitlement to have the confidentiality of his personal information preserved is derived from a right to privacy, then the patient's desire to keep certain information confidential should be respected even though in doing so the patient's own interests may be harmed.

But can all patients be regarded as autonomous for the purposes of all decisions such as these? Does a child patient have the same right to confidentiality as her parents, for example?[35] While it is submitted that the child patient has the same right to privacy as do her parents by virtue of her status as a member of the human race, at the same time the doctor treating a child may often have to override any strict obligation of confidentiality on the grounds that otherwise the child may very well not receive the care that she needs. It would be ludicrous to suggest that a doctor should not discuss a toddler's illness and the treatment that she requires with her mother. But children grow and begin to express a wish to control aspects of their own lives. When should a medical practitioner faced with a child patient decide that the child's wish to have total confidence preserved should prevail? It appears that there is no single answer to this question. One child may reach the capacity to make autonomous decisions long before others of her peer group. Any fixed age in law at which autonomy is recognised ignores this reality. This was the issue faced by the House of Lords in the case of Mrs Victoria Gillick.[36] Mrs Gillick sought an assurance from her local health authority that her daughters would not be given advice concerning contraception and abortion without her consent. The authority refused to give the assurance, and Mrs Gillick sought a declaration from the court that the authority's decision and the guidelines of the DHSS on which the authority's refusal was based were unlawful. She was unsuccessful in her application. The approach taken in the House of Lords was that while the age of consent for medical treatment was 16, nevertheless,

> As a matter of law parental right to determine whether or not their minor child below the age of 16 will have medical treatment terminates if and when the child achieves a sufficient understanding and intelligence to understand fully what is proposed . . . It will be a question of fact whether a child seeking advice has sufficient understanding of what is involved to give a consent valid in law.[37]

Thus for the law relating to consent to treatment the test was the maturity of the child patient. The decision in *Gillick* did not directly address the issue of confidentiality, and it has been suggested that the precise position is uncertain.[38] The suggestion has been made by Jonathan Montgomery that decision-making capacity is decision-relative.[39] A child may possess the competency to make one particular decision in relation to her health but lack the capacity in relation to another decision. In view of these considerations the medical practitioner should think long and hard before he decides to break the confidentiality of a child patient on the ground that such a breach is in the child's interests. The sceptical medical practitioner on reading the above may wish to argue that the obligation may be all very well, but what if he is faced with a child seeking treatment who he discovers has been sexually abused? Should silence be maintained if the child does not want anyone else to know?

Ultimately it is for the medical practitioner to judge if his patient possesses the capacity to make an autonomous decision to the effect that his medical information should be kept confidential. In the case of a child patient it is not a decision which should be taken lightly (in the situation outlined above, faced with an abused child the doctor may feel constrained to break confidence not only in the interests of the child but also in the public interest. The scope of the public-interest exception is discussed below).

Information the disclosure of which is required by statute or by court order

There is no general duty in law to inform the police regarding crime. In *Rice v Connolly* (1966)[40] Lord Justice Parker held that 'It seems to me quite clear that though every citizen has a moral duty, or if you like a social duty to assist the police, there is no legal duty to this effect.'[41] The law stipulates that in various circumstances the patient's confidential medical information must be disclosed by the doctor. For example if a doctor treats a patient suffering from a notifiable disease such as cholera, smallpox or typhus, he must send to the proper officer of the local authority a certificate giving details of the patient and of the disease from which he is suffering.[42] A doctor who terminates a pregnancy is required to give notice within seven days to the Chief Medical Officer.[43] Under the Road Traffic Act 1988 any person if so requested by the police has a duty to give information which might lead to the identification of a person who has committed an offence under the Act. The doctor is required to provide a patient's name and address, but does not have to provide clinical details.[44] The doctor is also subject to the provisions of the Prevention of Terrorism (Temporary Provisions) Act 1989.[45] Failure to give information which may be of material assistance in preventing the commission of certain acts of violence for political ends constitutes an offence.

If the police require other medical information for the purposes of carrying out their investigations than is covered by the limited provisions of the Road Traffic Act and which does not relate to the offence of terrorism included within the Prevention of Terrorism Act 1989, they can rely on the provisions of the Police and Criminal Evidence Act 1984.[46] This Act spells out in detail the powers of the police to search and seize premises for evidence to assist with their investigations. When the Government first put forward their proposals the BMA were severely critical, and they argued that there should be special protection for medical information in the same way as was being proposed for confidential information relating to legal matters. The original proposals, they suggested, would lead to defensive practices on the part of doctors such as deliberately refraining from keeping full and accurate medical histories of their patients. It was imperative that before access was allowed the police should be required to show a very strong justification indeed. In response to the criticism the Government included medical information in a small class of material which was given special protection under the Act. Unlike material subject to legal professional privilege, such information is not subject to automatic exclusion from the powers which the Act provides. Nevertheless, the claim by the police for disclosure of medical information will be subject to greater scrutiny than usual where evidence is requested. Before access is allowed to premises such as a doctor's surgery or to a hospital to search for medical records or samples of human tissue or tissue fluid taken for diagnosis or medical treatment or held in confidence, application must be made to a circuit judge for a warrant. Before the judge the police officer must show that the criteria of schedule 1 of the Act are satisfied. There must be a reasonable belief that the information he needs is contained on the premises and that prior to the 1984 Act a statute existed under which he could have obtained that information. How much of a safeguard to confidentiality these provisions are may be questioned. There is no duty upon the police when applying for a warrant to inform the person whom the confidential information concerns regarding the application for the warrant; only the person who is holding the information, in the case of hospital medical records, a hospital administrator. If the obligation of confidentiality is owed to the patient, it is arguable that the patient should have a voice at the hearing.[47]

There is as yet little indication as to what extent the section has provided a safeguard to confidential medical information in practice. One heartening example of the use of the section is provided by the Medical Defence Union. A haematologist was approached by the police. A murder had taken place and the only real clue to the offence was provided by blood found at the scene of the crime. The police asked the haematologist to give them a list of the names and addresses of all males of that particular blood group in that area. The haematologist took advice from the Medical Defence Union and refused to disclose the information.[48] The police sought a warrant from a circuit judge, who refused their application on the grounds that this would have amounted to 'trawling' through the medical records of some 1,000 males. It is to be hoped that such judicial restraint is characteristic of future interpretations of the section.

There is another problem in relation to the search and seizure provisions in PACE, and that concerns the operation of section 19. While the police must usually obtain a search warrant, once they are lawfully on premises they may, by virtue of this section, seize anything which constitutes evidence of an offence: there is no need for a special search warrant. The General Medical Council provide that information may also be legitimately disclosed where this is in pursuance of an order of the court.

The doctor's duty to society

Most commentators are in agreement that there are some situations in which the doctor's obligation to preserve the ethic of confidentiality is overridden by the interests of the public at large.[49] Yet the precise point at which private rights are outweighed by the public interest has been the subject of considerable debate. Widespread erosion of confidentiality on the grounds of the interests of society at large is, it is suggested, very dangerous. If pushed to extremes, it would almost totally undermine the practitioner's ethical obligation. Yet, it is clear that some breaches of confidentiality in the public interest are justified. There is unanimity among medical practitioners with whom I have discussed the subject, that if they were faced with a patient who was a psychopath they would have no hesitation in breaking confidentiality because of the clear danger that such a person poses to the rest of the population. Outside such a clear-cut situation, however, there is considerable disagreement.

Generally the public interest in breach of confidence concerns two categories of cases:

1 those where, by breaking confidence, the doctor is able to avoid harm in the form of physical injury being caused to others; and
2 those where the disclosure will avoid the 'harm' in the form of a guilty person being able to escape punishment because his crime remains undetected.

Where the patient suffers from an illness which is of a nature which could lead to injury to others, then some commentators argue that disclosure in the public interest is justified. Epilepsy accounts for more than half the instances of a driver being found unconscious at the wheel of his car. Mason and McCall Smith suggest that if a doctor is treating a patient who suffers from epilepsy and the patient refuses to inform the Driving and Vehicle Licensing Centre at Swansea about his condition, a positive moral duty is imposed on the doctor to inform the Licensing Centre about his patient's condition.[50] In view of the dangers of drinking and driving it is interesting to speculate on the extent to which there is a positive moral duty on a medical practitioner today to break confidence if faced with an alcoholic patient who the doctor is quite aware is still driving. Should the doctor tell the police?

If, when carrying out a routine medical examination, a doctor discovers that his patient is suffering from hypertension and fears that this could be dangerous to others since the patient is an airline pilot, the doctor is again placed in a difficult dilemma. If he were a company doctor he would owe a duty to the company to disclose those details, but should a GP disclose that information to the airline if the pilot refuses to do so? The disclosure would amount to a breach of the ethical obligation owed to his patient, and yet failure to disclose could lead to a major disaster. Beauchamp and Childress give an example of one case in which a psychiatrist used hypnotic techniques to help a pilot recall information about his responsibility for the crash of a commercial plane.[51] This information indicated that the pilot should not fly for at least a temporary period. The therapist was unable to convince the pilot, and he returned to work. Six months later he made an error of judgment which led to the crash of a plane on a transatlantic flight and the loss of many lives. In such a situation was the therapist right not to disclose the information?

Very controversial questions involving the extent of the duty to society exception concern those instances where the doctor discovers that a patient has committed or is about to commit a criminal offence.

Freeling and Harris give the example of a woman who goes to her doctor, complaining of anxiety. She says that her 17-year-old son had been charged with vandalising an empty house and that while she and her husband had given him an alibi they had lied and that they knew that their son had been involved. She asks the doctor to speak to the boy. The doctor later does so and the boy admits the offence. Should the doctor disclose the information? It has been suggested that if a doctor goes ahead and breaks confidentiality, disclosing that a patient has committed a crime, he will come within the duty to society exception that disclosure was justifiable on the grounds that it would prevent the harm of a crime being committed. But does this depend upon the type of crime? If a serious crime such as rape or murder has been committed, then the situation concerning whether to break confidence would appear comparatively clear. Breach of confidence in respect of lesser offences such as road traffic offences and shoplifting is less likely to be justified.

A recent example of the dilemma which may face a practitioner as to whether he should disclose a crime was mentioned in the *Journal of the Medical Defence Union*.[52] A burglar attempting to escape from the scene of the crime was injured during a car chase with the police. He was taken to hospital. Initially he was placed under police guard, but this was removed since he seemed unlikely to abscond. However, the burglar did abscond, with chest drains intact! A doctor to whom the burglar came for treatment wanting an assurance of complete confidentiality might be faced with a very difficult decision. The crime would almost certainly be revealed during their consultation. Whether he should disclose that information is by no means ethically clear.

The problem of whether the 'interests of society' require disclosure is particularly acute in cases where the patient has not yet committed an offence but it is feared that he may, whether because of his personality traits or his declared intention. Take, for instance, the case of a 26-year-old single man discussed by Langton and Torby.[53] He had been referred to a psychiatrist and then to the Regional Forensic Psychiatry service. He declared that during the past year he had attempted sexual assaults upon several different women but that these had been unsuccessful. All the women were unknown to him. The man had suffered an unhappy childhood and had a complicated psychological history and many of the characteristics of a psychopathic personality. The patient wanted strict confidentiality. Allowing voluntary treatment to continue would mean that there was a chance that the patient could harm another woman, yet to break confidentiality could have broken up the therapist–patient relationship. In this case confidentiality was preserved and a successful course of therapy was pursued. Not all medical practitioners, however, even in the area of psychiatric medicine, are prepared to take that risk, and if they believe that the patient may injure others, they may break confidence. Take the example of Dr Egdell which I discussed above.[54] For the purpose of compiling a report for a Mental Health Review Tribunal hearing, Dr Egdell examined a patient held in a secure hospital after killing five persons. The report revealed that W, the patient, probably had a psychopathic deviant personality and that W expressed an interest in fireworks, by which W meant tubes of steel piping packed with chemicals. After W's solicitors received the report they decided to withdraw W's application to the tribunal. Dr Egdell, however, considered that a report should be placed on W's file and a copy was sent to the hospital and to the Home Office.

The devastating consequences of what may happen if a doctor does not break confidence were shown dramatically in the case of *Tarasoff v Regents of the University of California*.[55] Poddar was a university student who sought out-patient treatment in a psychiatric hospital. He was suffering from deep depression as a result of being rejected by a Miss Tarasoff, with whom he had fallen in love. He told a psychologist at the hospital of his intention to kill Miss Tarasoff. After discussions with two psychiatrists, the psychologist decided that

Poddar should be detained in a mental hospital. He informed the campus police, who detained Poddar but later released him when he appeared to be rational. Two months after the consultation with the psychologist Poddar killed Miss Tarasoff. The majority in the Californian Supreme Court held that the defendant therapist was under a duty to warn the victim and the victim's family and was liable for his failure to do so.

The Tarasoff decision led to an outcry from psychiatric associations in the United States. They argued that the obligation was contrary to the therapist's obligation to ensure his patient's welfare by compromising confidentiality. In addition it asked them to predict the unpredictable, namely the likelihood of future violence.[56] The opposition led the court to reconsider their decision, and some eighteen months later the court held that the duty upon therapists was not that they should warn the victim but one of exercising reasonable care for the victim's protection. The court said that:

> The discharge of this duty may require the therapist to take one or more of various steps depending on the nature of the case. Thus it may call for him to warn the intended victim or other likely to apprise the victim of the danger, to notify the police, or to take whatever steps are reasonably necessary under the circumstances . . . The protective privilege ends when the public peril begins.[57]

Tarasoff has been followed in other cases.[58] There were echoes of it in the judgment of Scott J in *W v Egdell*, a judgment which was given approval by Sir Stephen Brown in the Court of Appeal. Scott J said that:

> In my view a doctor called upon as Dr Egdell was to examine a patient owes a duty not only to his patient but also a duty to the public. His duty to the public would require him in my opinion to place before the proper authorities the results of his examination if in his opinion the public interest so requires.

These words have potentially very worrying consequences. Will this lead to the English courts being prepared to find that a doctor owes a duty of care to the person his patient claims he is going to kill or seriously injure? The exception on the grounds of the interests of society is wide. It may provide a doctor with a defence in an action for breach of confidence and still not overbear the right to privacy of patients generally to any great extent. But, if the 'shield' is turned into a 'sword', to borrow terminology from another area of law, then this may have considerable repercussions for individual privacy if medical practitioners feel constrained to divulge to ensure that they do not become liable in tort.[59] In the United States there is evidence that *Tarasoff* has had that type of impact, leading more people to disclose information. Bowers, Givelber and Blitch have written that there was 'a widespread endorsement of the *Tarasoff* obligation to protect potential victims as personal and professional norms'.

The fact that the medical profession recognise that the patient's interest in preserving confidentiality may be outweighed by other interests does not by itself mean that the patient's right to confidentiality has been devalued – simply that it is outweighed in certain situations. In some circumstances the right to privacy is overborne by weightier interests. But if the public interest is used overmuch to justify such breaches then it will be highly questionable to what extent confidentiality is more rhetoric than reality.

Information required for the purposes of a medical research project approved by an ethical committee

If a patient's medical information is required for the purposes of research, then as long as the research has been approved by an ethical committee this information can be obtained without the patient's consent. The Lindop Committee did not regard this as a serious inroad upon the patient's rights because the person to whom the information had been passed, the research physician, was himself bound by an obligation of confidence and thus the actual breach was little more than technical.[60] Yet is it right to say that this obligation is truly the same as that which normally arises in the standard physician–patient relationship? Huw W. S. Francis argues that it is not.[61] The research physician's aim is that of achieving a successful research project. He intends to benefit not the patient who is part of that study but rather those who may succumb to the particular illness and become patients in future. He argues that this breach of confidence is divergent, because it does not fall within a known group of continuing professional commitments. If Francis is correct, then the increase in medical research can be viewed as a threat to patient confidentiality.

The bond of confidence which exists between practitioner and patient is not severed by the existence of exceptions to the general obligation. But the medical profession need to remain vigilant to ensure that the exceptions are not allowed to expand to an extent which makes the rule itself little more than rhetoric. Perhaps a greater threat to the ethic comes not from 'authorised exceptions', since the medical practitioner will usually consider carefully the implications of breaking complete confidentiality, but from what I now turn to consider, the unauthorised exceptions.

UNAUTHORISED EXCEPTIONS

Probably one of the greatest threats to patient confidentiality is posed by 'unauthorised breaches' of confidentiality. Such breaches are those which are neither necessary for the treatment of the patient nor sanctioned by the professional codes of conduct. These breaches are particularly harmful because, unlike other ways in which the obligation of confidentiality can be overridden, unauthorised breaches occur without a balanced rational decision having been made as to whether or not to disclose such information. If a doctor considers that it is in the interests of society that confidentiality should be broken, he will have come to this conclusion after weighing the harm that could accrue to the community at large by failing to break the patient's confidence. Unauthorised breaches, in contrast, are frequently the result of an accident or carelessness. Some medical practitioners have an unfortunate habit of discussing cases with which they have been recently involved at cocktail parties. It may be difficult for a doctor to keep total patient confidentiality by never discussing his cases with his family. Bloch and Chodoff comment that:

> When a psychiatrist is preoccupied by an anxiety causing case such as a suicidal patient, conflict exists between his wish to explain his preoccupation and his wish to protect the confidentiality of his patient, who may actually call and identify himself by name.[62]

Other medical information may be inadvertently disclosed during conversations with other patients. A practitioner may in the course of an examination tell a patient who is a university lecturer that he has only last week treated one of the lecturer's colleague's children for a similar back ailment. It is not uncommon for patients' records to be left lying around in hospitals. Weiss has written that in one Boston hospital 'rounds may be conducted in hallways and elevators' and that that seemed to be the practice in many hospitals.[63] Similarly, even practitioners in psychiatric medicine may break confidentiality by acting carelessly. Green saw it as ironic that a psychiatrist could write to a GP colleague who has referred a patient to him heading the letter 'private and confidential' when a list of six people to whom carbon copies had been sent was appended.[64] Some of these breaches may seem trivial – but breaches such as these illustrate the ease with which carelessness can erode the ethic. Medical practitioners may not appreciate the extent to which their patients expect them to keep confidence.

Unauthorised breaches may be the result of spite or malice. General practitioners rely to a considerable extent on their receptionists, who are usually drawn from the same local community which includes the GP's catchment area. There is a danger that a receptionist could take advantage of her ability to gain access to patients' medical records to pass on information maliciously about a patient to third parties. Similarly there is the potential for unauthorised breaches in hospitals to be carried out by laboratory, secretarial or other staff who are not bound by a professional code of ethics. An interesting example of an unauthorised breach of confidentiality is provided by Phillips and Dawson which also illustrates the level of disagreement among medical practitioners as to the precise extent of the obligation to their patient.[65] Martin Birnsting was a surgeon at St Bartholomew's Hospital in London. In 1979 one of his patients, a girl of Turkish Cypriot origin, aroused the suspicion of a clerk at the hospital that she might not be eligible for NHS treatment. She phoned the DHSS and confirmed with them that the girl was not entitled to treatment since she had overstayed her permit. The clerk told the surgeon about this and mentioned that it was a likely consequence that the girl would be arrested and deported. The surgeon was horrified and contacted the patient, telling her not to attend because he feared that she would be arrested. He complained publicly about this flagrant breach of confidentiality. The sequel to this was a letter to the *British Medical Journal* from another medical practitioner critical of Mr Birnsting: 'Mr Birnsting seems obsessed with confidentiality. Would he inform the police if a patient committed murder? Would Mr Birnsting break confidentiality to report a heroin pusher? Illegal immigrants and overstayers have only one legal right and that is deportation.' Breaches of confidentiality by hospital clerical staff can have devastating consequences, as this example shows.

Another danger to patient confidentiality has arisen as patient information is increasingly stored on computer: there is a potential for unauthorised access to data bases which contain patient information.[66] For example Family Practitioner Committee systems have been developed and have been implemented nationally. These contain comprehensive lists of NHS numbers, patient names and the previous and present general practitioners and Family Practitioner Committees to which patients have belonged. Health authorities have computerised registers which contain information about children. These contain notifications of births within the Health District and have been extended to cover immunisation, pre-school and school health modules. The establishment of these data bases was the subject of considerable controversy. The BMA argued that these measures were not accompanied by adequate privacy safeguards. The DHSS did agree to some safeguards as a result of lobbying, such as identifiable information not being used without the consent of the patient (or in the case of the child, the guardian of the child). But computerisation of sensitive information has continued. The Korner Committee, who recommended extensive computerisation of the NHS, included in their proposals a scheme for the computerisation of records in clinics involved in the treatment of sexually transmitted diseases.[67] This was to enable contact tracing to be more effective. Counsellors at these clinics try to persuade patients to identify recent sexual contacts who could have been infected by the disease. Campbell and Connor argued that in view of the AIDS crisis the creation of a computerised sexually transmitted disease contacts register is 'foolish and irresponsible'.[68] It would be equally foolish in the view of these writers were this form of registration to be extended to AIDS sufferers themselves, since this would facilitate authoritarian measures being introduced against such persons.

The dangers posed by computerised records are twofold. First, there is the possibility that patients' information may be transferred too freely within the Health Service itself, with the consequent threat that this poses to confidentiality. Recently the Data Protection Registrar, Mr Eric Howe, expressed his concern regarding computerised health-care records.[69] He stressed the problem of exactly who would have access to the data, in particular, whether administrators as opposed to health-care professionals would be able to identify individuals and all their health details. The Department of Health are presently working on non-statutory guidelines on confidentiality,[70] but the Data Protection Registrar argues that a statutory code of confidentiality is required.

Second, there is the possibility that persons who have no connection with the Health Service may be able to hack into the system and gain access to sensitive information. The repercussions of hackers gaining access to sensitive personal information concerning children, for example, may be very grave indeed. The ease by which access can be gained to such computer systems can be well illustrated by reference to computer hacking both in this country and in the United States. In 1983 a computer systems manager at New York City Hospital discovered that various patients' medical records had been destroyed. One computer which had been monitoring therapy had failed, and the records were destroyed by a computer hacker who had broken into the system after learning the pass word.[71] In this country during the debate on the Computer Misuse Act 1990 it was revealed that the medical records of one HIV-positive patient had been accessed through hacking and that the patient had been subjected to blackmail as a result, and also that cancer patients had had their records accessed.[72] It remains to be seen how far the criminalisation of computer hacking will operate as a deterrent to would-be hackers.

CONCLUSIONS

Phillips and Dawson argue that confidentiality should be upheld because a doctor who abuses the trust and confidence which his patient imposes on him is behaving in a dishonest manner. This is not to say that confidentiality is sacrosanct. As we have seen, such a view of medical confidentiality is not taken by the medical profession today. What I have attempted to show in this chapter is that there is a *prima facie* presumption of confidentiality but that there is considerable potential for it to be overridden and that the medical profession are aware of this. This lack of a standard approach to confidentiality prompts the suggestion that a privilege should also not protect confidentiality in a uniform manner. The law should avoid a situation in which confidentiality is upheld in court but the same information is freely available in practice. It was mentioned earlier that many are now of the view that little medical information is truly confidential but that that which is so confidential should remain so. The law should target protection at those patients who have requested that their personal medical information remain undisclosed or that it be disclosed only to a limited extent. The areas of psychiatry and psychotherapy seem to lend themselves to such protection, as do those doctor–patient relationships in which the parties have agreed that the information should remain in confidence. Exactly how a privilege statute could be drawn up to protect such confidential information is the subject of the next chapter.

5

PRACTICAL PROBLEMS IN PRIVILEGE ENACTMENT

We may believe that the patient has a right to confidentiality which justifies him in stopping his medical information from being disclosed in the courtroom. But by itself, that is not enough. We need to go on and consider just how far that right should be applied in law. In this chapter I attempt to put some flesh upon the bare bones of theory. The various component parts of an evidential privilege statute are assembled and their precise form and extent are discussed. Should, for example, the privilege apply to all types of litigation, or should criminal cases be excluded? Which medical practitioners should be included within privilege protection? My general practitioner is an obvious candidate for inclusion, but what about my osteopath or my homeopathic practitioner? Should a privilege apply to protect my confidences to my doctor when I am in my grave? These types of questions both are of practical interest to lawyers and also raise important issues relating to the scope of medical practice today. Readers may find it helpful to refer back at this point to the conclusions of chapter 3 before proceeding further.

THE SCOPE OF THE PRIVILEGE

There are four possible alternative ways in which a medical professional privilege statute could be enacted.

Option 1 is that of enacting an evidential privilege covering the relationship between the psychiatrist and his patient while not including other doctor–patient relationships. This type of division has taken place in certain jurisdictions within the United States. The problem with this approach is that it ignores the indisputable fact that other doctor–patient relationships are highly confidential. No one surely would be prepared to deny that the patient being treated for venereal disease or for AIDS should be unable to argue that his treatment was not worthy of just as much protection as the disclosures made on the psychiatrist's couch. This option should not be followed. Option 2 is the inclusion of all medical practitioner–patient relationships within a privilege statute. But this would have the effect of protecting all doctor–patient relationships, even though it would be unrealistic to regard them all as equally 'confidential'. I noted earlier how, for example, a patient with a broken leg would be unlikely to regard his condition as confidential. A situation could arise in which a patient could take refuge behind a privilege when the information was not imparted in confidence.

Option 3 is the adoption of a discretionary approach. At present there is no wide general exclusionary discretion in English law which enables a judge to take account of broad policy considerations before allowing evidence to be admitted (although, as we have seen, in criminal cases there may now be scope for argument that section 78 of the Police and Criminal Evidence Act 1984 has some application). The judge may exert pressure on counsel not to push a particular question, but when it comes to the 'forensic crunch' it is law that is in command, and the evidence should be disclosed.

In Canada and Australia, various law-reform bodies have suggested that flexible exclusionary rules should be enacted to cover all professional relationships.[1] The advantage of a discretionary approach is that it would enable the court to differentiate between those relationships which were clearly confidential and those which were not. But certain drawbacks exist, which these law-reform bodies fail to discuss in their reports. The court in determining whether or not to exclude communications would need to assess at the very least whether these were transmitted in confidence. This could simply be a matter of the court accepting the word of the medical practitioner as to their confidential quality, thus avoiding the need to consider the nature of the relationships and the communications in considerable detail. But if a dispute arose between doctor and patient concerning whether the communications were 'confidential', problems could result.

In determining the confidential quality of the information the judge should place considerable weight upon any agreement which has been reached as a result of negotiation between the parties. But a dispute would almost invariably arise if the parties had failed to reach agreement through negotiation or more likely if there had been no negotiation at all. In such a situation it would fall to the court to review the nature of the communications in detail. Such a review would seem particularly undesirable as far as psychiatrist–patient communications were concerned in view of their inherently sensitive nature.

Option 4 is a combination of options 1 and 3. The psychiatrist–patient relationship should be afforded a full privilege, such recognition reflecting the high level of confidentiality within that relationship. But for the standard doctor–patient relationship with its sliding scale of confidentiality a form of discretionary test is a better solution. The court could examine whether the relationship was truly confidential. This alternative has of course the attendant problems of option 3 as regards the operation of a discretion. But it is suggested that of the alternatives the fourth option is preferable. While it will mean that the court will on occasion have to examine medical evidence to determine its confidential quality, it is an improvement upon the blanket approach of option 2, which could have the effect of excluding evidence that was in no way 'confidential'.

CIVIL, CRIMINAL OR BOTH?

At present the exclusionary rules of privilege and public policy in English law apply to both civil and to criminal cases. This does not preclude a different approach from being taken as far as a medical professional privilege is concerned. In several other jurisdictions which already possess such a privilege either the privilege is expressed to be applicable only in civil litigation or there have been attempts by the court to curtail the extent of its application in criminal cases. The right to keep medical information confidential should, it was suggested earlier, be capable of being overborne in certain situations. I do not propose to repeat the arguments in full, and so will merely state the conclusions which I reached. The right to privacy is overborne in a case when it comes into conflict with the right of the defendant to place before the court evidence necessary to substantiate his innocence in a criminal trial. Similarly there is a weighty public-interest consideration which justifies the production of medical evidence where this is essential for the prosecution of those who have committed grave crimes and in those cases in which the welfare of a child may be in issue. Litigation involving children is an emotive subject. There is a clear public interest in ensuring that a child is not subjected to the dangers of abuse by others and that a child is properly cared for.

Although there is a clear public interest that evidence should be excluded in certain cases, that does not necessarily mean that the privilege should be totally removed in all those cases relating to child welfare or the prosecution of a grave crime. One alternative would be to allow the judge to decide whether the privilege should be overridden on a case-by-case basis with reference to a list of specified criteria. Such an approach has been suggested by the Australian Law Reform Commission.[2] They propose that the judge be directed to take into account whether the proceedings were criminal and whether the party which wanted to adduce the evidence was the prosecution or the defendant and the nature of the subject matter of the proceedings. In addition the judge is to have the power to exclude confidential communications made or compiled in furthering the commission of a fraud or an offence or an act which would make a person liable to a criminal penalty. I suggest that the problem with such a test is that it includes too many variables and would be a recipe for undesirable uncertainty.

A threshold test has been used in the English law of evidence in an area where it has been thought important that access to evidence be limited. The Sexual Offences (Amendment) Act 1976 provides in section 2 (1) that in a rape trial details of the sexual history of the complainant other than with the defendant cannot be adduced as evidence without the leave of the judge. The section goes on to provide that:

> (2) The judge shall not give leave in pursuance of the preceding subsection for the evidence or question except on an application made to him in the absence of the jury by or on behalf of the defendant; and on such an application the judge shall give leave if and only if he is satisfied that it would be unfair to that defendant to refuse to allow the evidence to be adduced or the question to be asked.

The court in deciding whether a privilege should be overridden should be concerned to assess whether that evidence was truly needed. Perhaps the guidelines laid down by the court in *R v Lawrence* (1977)[3] in interpreting s.2 (1) may be appropriate. In that case May J said that:

> before a judge is satisfied . . . that to refuse to allow a particular question or a series of questions in cross examination would be unfair to a defendant he must take the view that it is more likely

than not that the particular question or line of cross-examination, if allowed, might reasonably lead the jury, properly directed in the summing up, to take a different view of the complainant's evidence from that which they might take if the question or series of questions was or were not allowed.[4]

Applying this approach in the context of medical privilege, if a defendant in a criminal trial wanted the admission of medical evidence in order to establish his innocence, he should be required to show that the evidence was essential for his case such that the court might reasonably take a substantially different view of the evidence before them if the privilege were not waived. Similarly if the prosecution in a murder trial wanted to adduce evidence to show that one of two defendants was the more likely to have committed an offence, they would need to show that without the evidence there was a reasonable possibility that the jury might take a substantially different view of the guilt or innocence of the defendants.

INFORMATION COVERED BY THE PRIVILEGE

Communications

Kottow has written that:

In consulting a doctor a person implicitly accepts the risk of surrendering more information than intended but at the same time understands herself or himself to be under the protection of confidentiality. Information fortuitously gained within the freely chosen association of the clinical encounter is to be considered confidential and treated in the same way as information voluntarily disclosed by the patient.[5]

If there is agreement as to the fact that doctor–patient communications should be privileged, we need to ask ourselves before we go any further precisely which communications should be privileged. Are they restricted to what the patient himself tells the doctor, or do they include the conclusions reached by the doctor about the patient's medical condition or the results of tests which the doctor has performed?

Different definitions have been used in different jurisdictions. In Australia a narrow interpretation was given to the scope of the privilege. For example in *Lucenea v National Mutual Life Association of Australia* (1912) Lewis LJ held that 'communications' referred to those statements made by the patient to the doctor concerning facts about the patient's medical condition of which the patient himself is aware.[6] They did not extend to cover those facts which were observed through the doctor carrying out an examination. While the minority in the case took a somewhat broader approach, the approach of the majority was reflected in the Evidence Amendment Act 1982.

This broader approach is akin to that adopted in the United States. Wigmore divided communications into 'active communications' – verbal exchanges between doctor and patient – and 'passive' communications, which take the form of observations made by the doctor about the physical condition of the patient.[7] Comments made in decided cases in the United States reflect this approach. In *Burns v Waterloo* (1870), a personal injury case, it was held that the physician could not testify as to the fact that when treating the patient he had seen that he was intoxicated.[8] In *Briggs v Briggs* (1874) it was said that the privilege covered 'whatever was disclosed to any of his senses and which in any way was brought to his knowledge for that purpose',[9] and in *Gartside v Ins* (1882) it was held that 'information acquired by a physician from inspection, examination or observation of the patient' is equally privileged.[10]

The broad interpretation of communications as covering both active and passive communications to the doctor is preferable. The patient's personal information surely includes his physical condition as revealed to the doctor during the course of an examination as much as the patient's own, often rather incoherent, description of his symptoms. Privilege should also be extended to cover the patient's medical records. While the record is not composed entirely of information emanating from the patient, nevertheless most of the information does derive either directly or indirectly from him. It would be practically very difficult for the court to make a distinction between the facts of the patient's condition and the subjective opinion of the medical practitioner contained in the patient's records. Furthermore, it would be exceedingly unusual for a patient's medical records to be excluded, especially in view of the fact that the Access to Health Records Act 1990 provides a statutory right of access. Any privilege statute should be drafted liberally and the patient's records included.

Should samples of blood and other body fluids taken from the patient by his doctor in the course of a medical examination be included within the privilege? A sample taken from a patient, may, when analysed, give the doctor a better indication of the patient's current state of health than the patient's own description of his symptoms or a clinical examination. Interestingly, in a case decided prior to the enactment of the Police and Criminal Evidence Act 1984, *R v Apicella* (1986),[11] the court refused to exercise a discretion to exclude evidence of samples which the defendant, unbeknown to the doctor, had been forced to give. The claim that these samples were in effect analogous to a confession and that they should therefore be given special recognition for the purposes of the law of evidence was rejected. Now under the Police and Criminal Evidence Act 1984, samples have been accorded a special position in one respect in that they have been classed as 'excluded material' where they have been taken for the purposes of diagnosis and medical treatment and are held in confidence.[12] However, as far as those samples taken from the defendant while he is in custody are concerned, a different approach has been taken. Samples have been divided into two categories: intimate samples, which may be taken from the defendant only as long as consent is given,[13] and non-intimate samples, which may be taken from the defendant regardless of consent.[14] Intimate samples are defined as being 'a sample of blood, semen, or any other tissue fluid, urine, saliva or pubic hair or a swab taken from a person's body orifice'.[15] Intimate samples may not be taken without the consent of the suspect, although, should he refuse to let the sample be taken without showing good reason for his refusal, this may be used as evidence against him in later court proceedings.[16] Non-intimate samples may, however, be taken without consent.

I suggest that such samples should be regarded as being as much 'communications' between doctor and patient as any clinical examination. That would not mean that all samples would be capable of being excluded as privileged. Exclusion would depend upon whether or not they amounted to confidential communications for the purposes of medical treatment, which is an issue I now turn to.

Confidential

It has been suggested that communications between doctor and patient should not be privileged unless they are 'confidential'. But just what is meant by 'confidential communications'? This is something which could be left to the judiciary to interpret on a case-by-case basis. However, there is an advantage in at least some general form of definition: that of promoting consistency between decisions. But drafting such a definition is no straightforward task. Some might regard confidential information as information transmitted between two people, the recipient promising not to reveal it to others. Other definitions have been considerably wider and are perhaps of more assistance to us here in that they do reflect the realities of modern-day medical practice far more closely. In the United States Rule 504 of the proposed Federal Rules of Evidence, which incorporated a psychotherapist–patient privilege, stipulated that communications were to be 'confidential'

> (i) if not intended to be disclosed to third persons other than those present to further the interest of the patient in the consultation, examination or interview, or persons reasonably necessary for the transmission of the communications or persons who are participating in the diagnosis and treatment under the direction of the psychotherapist including members of the patient's family.[17]

This type of definition has the advantage of taking into account the fact that the patient is unlikely to be treated by only one medical practitioner, particularly over a long period of treatment, or if the patient is to be referred to a hospital specialist. Some modification of Rule 504 is necessary because that rule was designed specifically for psychotherapist–patient communications. The following phrasing may perhaps be more appropriate:

> A communication is confidential if it is not intended to be disclosed to third persons other than those persons present to further the interests of the patient in consultation or examination or persons reasonably necessary for the transmission of the communication or persons who are involved in the diagnosis and treatment of the patient under the direction of the doctor. In determining the confidential quality of the information, weight should be placed upon any agreement between the practitioner and the patient as to which information should be treated as confidential.

This approach would have the effect that the consultation at which a junior doctor or a nurse was present would still come within a privilege statute. To exclude the application of the privilege simply because a nurse was present would be highly unrealistic, even if the nurse–patient relationship may not yet be fully included within a privilege statute, as we shall see later. The inclusion of the provision that communications may still be confidential if a person is present who is reasonably necessary for the communication to take place is deliberate. Such a situation would arise when a doctor faced with a patient brought into hospital who is unable to communicate adequately in English calls in an interpreter. If the presence of the interpreter is necessary for the consultation to go ahead, it should not devalue the confidential quality of the information. One possible problem with such a definition arises in the context of group psychotherapy, in which problems are discussed in a group setting. Later in this chapter I suggest that practitioners of psychotherapy should only be included within a privilege statute if they are registered medical practitioners. If such a person led a therapy session, then could a privilege later be invoked to prevent the disclosures which have taken place during the therapy session from being revealed? I suggest that the definition which I have provided justifies such inclusion since the presence of other members of the group during the therapy session is necessary for therapy to take place. The privilege should in this situation be invoked to stop other members of the group from testifying regarding confidential information communicated during the clinical encounter.

There is one further issue. If a patient's confidential information is disclosed by a medical practitioner to a third party outside the courtroom and then later at trial the patient decides that he wants to assert the privilege, should he be entitled to claim it as confidential? This perhaps depends upon the context. If the information has been disclosed without any justification, then surely it would be wrong to disclose it. The patient should not be penalised for his doctor's trangression. But if the doctor discloses outside the courtroom and this disclosure *is* justifiable, then should this evidence be admitted? In many situations this type of disclosure would be justifiable by reference to one of the exceptions already built into a privilege statute. The doctor's decision to inform the victim of the defendant's declared intention to harm her would be sanctioned outside the court both by the public-interest defence and by the medical profession's ethical code. Evidence of the doctor about what the patient had told him during the consultation would also surely be admissible if it could be shown by the prosecution that the evidence was 'essential' for the prosecution of a grave crime.

There is a problem, however, if an existing statute required disclosure but the information in question did not come within one of the recognised exceptions to the general rule of privilege outlined in chapter 3. To avoid potential conflict between the privilege statute and existing statutes there are two alternative approaches which could be taken. The first is that a radical overhaul of those statutes could be made in order to determine the extent to which they were justifiable. This is a study which, as I suggested in chapter 4, was too wide-ranging for the purposes of this book but is one which should perhaps be undertaken in the future. The second and less controversial option is to hold that where a conflict exists between the privilege and existing statutes the privilege should be held inapplicable. Of these two options I tentatively suggest that the first is preferable.

For the purposes of medical treatment

Medical privilege statutes have long contained the limitation that, in order for privilege protection to apply, communications between doctor and patient must be 'for the purposes of medical treatment'. So, for example, the early privilege statute in New York State provided that:

> No person duly authorised to practice physic or surgery shall be allowed to disclose any information which he may have acquired in attending the patient in a professional character and which information was necessary to enable him to prescribe for such a patient as physician or to act for him as surgeon.[18]

This limitation was consistent with the professed aim of the early privilege statutes, that of ensuring that the individual is not discouraged from seeking treatment by the fear of disclosure.[19] Similar wording is to be found in the most recent privilege statute of New York State:

> Unless the patient waives the privilege a person authorised to practice medicine, registered professional nursing, licenced practical nursing, dentistry or chiropractic shall not be allowed to disclose any information which he acquired in attending the patient in a professional capacity and which was necessary for him to act in that capacity.[20]

But, how applicable is that limitation to a privilege based upon the patient's right to privacy? It is indeed relevant, because the right to privacy has been regarded as being of particular weight here due to the fact that it is a professional relationship of confidence. Since there is a particular value in preserving the confidentiality of this professional relationship, it follows that any statute should only protect those communications made in confidence during that relationship.

This also means that the person who confides in a friend who happens to be a doctor will not be in a better position as far as privilege protection is concerned than the rest of the population. A further consequence of the limitation that to be privileged, communications must be made for the purposes of medical treatment is that reports ordered by a court for the purposes of legal proceedings will not be privileged since the primary aim of their production is not the care of the patient but the need to ensure that the wheels of the machinery of justice run smoothly.

In addition it appears that scope for the use of the privilege in the context of the operation of the Mental Health Act 1983 is extremely limited. The Mental Health Act 1983 provides that persons who are suffering from 'mental disorder' or from mental illness may be admitted into hospital for assessment or for treatment, and specifies that reports are required from medical practitioners for this purpose.[21] Similar provisions for reports to be made exist in relation to those patients accused in criminal cases and who it is believed suffer from some form of mental disorder to determine whether they are fit to stand trial.[22] While this type of information relating as it does to the treatment of individuals would, *prima facie*, be of the type of information to be privileged, it would fall outside the privilege statute because it was not 'for the purposes of medical treatment'.

WHO SHOULD BE ABLE TO WAIVE THE PRIVILEGE?

Since the medical professional privilege outlined here is grounded in the patient's right to preserve the confidentiality of and to control access to his own personal information, it follows that the patient himself should be the one who is able to decide whether or not his personal information should be disclosed in court. Rather than forcing the patient to assert his privilege on each and every occasion, a statute should provide that the information is automatically privileged unless either, first, the patient decides that his medical information should be used as evidence and he waives the privilege or, second, the court holds that it falls within one of the exceptions recognised in the statute. This would have the benefit of reducing one of the 'costs' of the privilege, that of court proceedings being prolonged as a result of increased debate regarding the admission of evidence. This type of privilege statute has been enacted in other jurisdictions. A useful model is the medical privilege statute of the Australian state of Victoria, which provides that

> No physician or surgeon shall without the consent of his patient divulge in any civil action or proceeding (unless the sanity or testamentary capacity of the patient is the matter in dispute) any information which he acquired in attending the patient and which is necessary to enable him to prescribe and act for the patient.[23]

The doctor and his veto

General control of access to his medical information should lie in the hands of the patient. But should there be any exceptions to this? If the patient's doctor believes that disclosure of the patient's medical history in the courtroom could cause the patient harm, should he be able to veto the disclosure? In the United States there have been instances in which some practitioners have been prepared to go to jail rather than to give evidence, even after their patients have waived their privilege.[24] In Illinois the opposition to uncontrolled patient disclosure of medical information was so strong that the medical profession succeeded in obtaining an amendment to the state's privilege statute. The State of Illinois Evidence and Disposition Statute provides that the psychiatrist has a veto over whether he should testify concerning the patient's health.

Rather than basing their claim for a veto on the potential harm that disclosure might cause, some practitioners in America have suggested that their own right to privacy entitles them to refuse to testify. This argument was tested in the courts in the case of *Re Lifschutz* (1970).[25] Dr Lifschutz was a psychotherapist. One of his patients decided to waive his privilege and wanted the doctor to give evidence. Dr Lifschutz argued that his right to privacy entitled him to refuse. The court rejected his claim: 'It is the depth and intimacy of the patient's revelations that give rise to concern over compelled disclosure; the psychotherapist though undoubtedly deeply involved in the communicative treatment does not exert a significant privacy interest separate from his patient.' The court also considered the argument that compelled disclosure could harm successful therapy. Without the ability to assure patients that all revelations would be held in the strictest confidence the patients would, it was suggested, be prevented from participating fully in the psychotherapeutic process. The court said that although these issues raised by Dr Lifschutz were medical and non-legal, they took account of the fact that psychotherapy had grown and flourished in a climate of what was non-absolute privilege. His claim was dismissed.

Should an English privilege statute contain such a veto? If, as has been suggested above, a privilege should be based upon the right of the patient to control access to his own personal information, then a veto would deny that right. Such a right could be successfully overborne if there were a countervailing right/interest of sufficient strength. The medical practitioner's own claim right here is comparatively weak. He is not seeking to assert control over information concerning himself which is very confidential in its nature. The fact that he has been carrying out his role as a medical professional is surely not sensitive personal information. In essence the medical practitioner in claiming a veto of this type is acting paternalistically. Some might want to argue that public policy justifies the enactment of such a veto. There may be a public interest in preventing harm being caused to the patient. Such an argument is highly questionable. We should be very cautious about infringing the autonomy of the individual patient. In addition while the patient may cause himself harm by enforced disclosure, he may also cause himself harm by denying himself the damages which he might otherwise have been able to obtain through that disclosure. Ultimately the patient's right to choose when disclosure takes place should prevail.

The patient litigant exception

If a patient puts his medical condition into issue, then the court may say that by doing so he has 'waived' his privilege. The justification advanced for this is that a patient should not be able to submit a claim or defence based upon his ill health and then be able to use his privilege as a means of preventing the other party from putting forward available conflicting evidence. As Wigmore has argued:

> The whole reason for the privilege is the patient's supposed unwillingness that the ailment should be disclosed to the world at large, hence the bringing of a suit in which the very declaration and much more the proof discloses the ailment to the world at large is of itself an indication that the supposed repugnancy to disclosure does not exist.[26]

The patient–litigant exception exists in the United States, where most jurisdictions have some form of medical privilege. This exception usually provides that once the patient has placed his mental or emotional condition in issue, then the medical practitioner can go ahead and testify without further consent from the patient.[27] This exception has merit. It is surely contrary to justice that the patient should be able to 'pick and choose' which parts of his medical evidence he decides to submit to the court, allowing access only to selected parts of his record while keeping back the rest, which may be contradictory or decisive to the case. Fairness points us in the direction of incorporating such an exception into English law.

Incompetence and privilege waiver

In three situations the patient is unable to waive his privilege. These are:

1 if the patient has died;
2 if the patient is a child and is unable to consent in any meaningful sense of the word to the waiver;
3 if the patient is suffering from illness or disability which is of a nature to impair his ability to reason.

Two questions will be addressed in this section. The first is whether we should allow medical evidence of patients falling into any one of these three categories to be admitted by allowing a third party to waive their privilege and, if so, who that third party should be.

The deceased patient

The obligation owed by the medical practitioner to his patient extends to keeping that confidence after the patient has died. If a doctor does reveal details about such a patient he will at the very least be the subject of considerable censure from his professional body, as we saw earlier in the case of Lord Moran, the surgeon who attended Winston Churchill.[28] Should a privilege statute reflect this element of medical practice? If the patient has expressly requested that his doctor should never disclose confidences which pass between them, it would be to deny the individual's right to control access to his own personal information for the doctor later to disclose information in the courtroom. More difficult is the more common situation in which the patient has expressed no desire as to whether his confidences should ever be disclosed.

We are faced with a difficult dilemma. Do we override the patient's confidentiality if the evidence is needed for the purpose of proceedings which arise after his death, even though he may have expressly stipulated absolute confidentiality? One approach is to argue that the individual's right to claim confidentiality for his personal information is one which is of less weight after his death. An analogy can be drawn with the law concerning defamation. The reputation of the individual is an important element in his life. But he loses the right to have that reputation safeguarded after his death by his descendants. I would disagree with such an argument. If a patient has entrusted personal information to his medical practitioner, then that doctor is bound to keep that confidence. It is indeed arguable that the obligation of confidence may be even more important after death because the patient no longer has any means by which he can dispute the assertions of his doctor.

Although the doctor–patient obligation of confidentiality is not severed on death, if blanket protection is given to confidentiality after death then this may have the effect of stultifying litigation. The number of situations in which the medical record of a deceased person is ever required as evidence is limited. But where it is of relevance it may be of some importance. In a murder trial the defendant may want the deceased's medical records to show that the deceased died not as a result of the defendant's actions but because of some intervening cause or other action such as suicide.[29] Where death is alleged to be the result of a tortious act of another, those who seek to bring a claim under the Law Reform Miscellaneous Provisions Act 1934 or the Fatal Accidents Act 1976 would require medical evidence to establish their claim that, for example, death was really caused by the accident brought about by the negligence of the defendant.[30] Evidence of the deceased's health would be essential for persons seeking to challenge the validity of a will on the grounds that the deceased was of unsound mind.[31] The problems of blanket protection of confidentiality after death are illustrated in some United States cases. In *Palmer v Order of United Commercial Travellers of America* (1932),[32] an action was brought to recover death benefits under a policy which excluded asphyxiation by carbon monoxide. A wife had found her husband lying on the floor with the car engine running. He had sustained bruises on his forehead and nose as a result of his collapse. Two doctors were summoned, but they were unable to revive him. At the hearing the doctors were called to testify that the face of the deceased had become cherry red as a result of carbon monoxide poisoning. The court, however, disallowed this evidence on the grounds that the information was privileged.

Similarly in *Re Flint* (1893)[33] privilege was applied to stop the admission of testimony of a doctor that he had prescribed for the 'mental treatment of his deceased patient'. The court held that it was important for the individual's privilege to remain inviolate beyond the grave.

Other United States courts rejected such an extreme view and were prepared to override the privilege on the grounds that justice must be done. In *Re Freeman* (1887) the court avoided the application of this rule by holding that no doctor–patient relationship was established.[34] The testatrix was examined by two doctors to determine her mental condition on the day that she made her will. Those doctors had never seen her before her last illness. It was held that since the doctor–patient relationship had not been established, the doctor's evidence that she was of sufficient mental capacity at that time was admissible. In *Sims v Charlotte Mutual Liberty Insurance Co.* (1962) the court were prepared to override the physician–patient privilege on the grounds that justice should be done.[35] The insurance company wanted to adduce hospital records to show that the deceased had made false claims on her life insurance policy. The court held that this evidence was material and that justice required it to be submitted.

In most United States jurisdictions today, statute provides that the privilege is inapplicable or that it may be waived in actions brought after the patient's death. For example in New York the Civil Practice Law and Rules provide that mental and physical information relating to the deceased patient may be disclosed if no objection is made to the admission of evidence, if privilege is waived by the personal representative of the deceased, or if the trial judge considers that it is in the interests of the estate that waiver should take place.[36] Wisconsin makes a similar provision: it provides that privilege, whether in the case of dead or living patients, does not apply if after the patient's death any party relies on the patient's condition as an element of his claim or defence.[37] To avoid courts in this country being tempted to follow the rather tenuous arguments advanced in *Re Freeman* and also to avoid resort being made by the courts to broad principles of justice to subvert the privilege as in *Sims* I suggest that any statute should clearly indicate the extent to which a privilege should apply after the death of the patient. There should be no automatic right to exclusion of a patient's medical information after his death. Protecting an individual's right to privacy should not be achieved at the cost of wiping out whole areas of litigation. One approach which might be adopted is that of deciding to waive the privilege on the grounds that the patient himself would have decided to waive it had he been still alive. But this type of test is exceedingly artificial. Unless we have some clear indication of how the patient regarded the confidentiality of his personal information after his death generally and in the context of particular litigation – a highly unlikely scenario – then the test would be unworkable. A better approach would be the adoption of a threshold test. If in an action brought after a deceased person's death the medical information of the deceased person was put into issue, then the judge should have power to waive the privilege if application of the privilege would lead to the court reasonably taking a substantially different view of the evidence before them than they would have taken had the privilege not been in operation.

The child

The right of the patient to control access to his own medical information may be a right which is both ethically justifiable and capable of being achieved in practice in the case of the adult patient. As far as children are concerned, though, it must be questioned to what extent we can realistically talk of the patient's right to regulate access to his medical information. It would be clearly ridiculous to talk of a baby exercising such a right. Yet as the child nears maturity, is he entitled to *de facto* control of his rights? It was noted in chapter 4 that children over 16 are legally competent to consent to medical treatment if a doctor is satisfied that they are sufficiently mature to do so.[38]

However, the extent to which the privilege statute needs to make special provision for the child patient is, it is suggested, doubtful. If the welfare of the child is at issue, then the privilege will be held inapplicable. If the child's mental or physical health is part of a claim advanced on behalf of the patient, then the privilege will be held to be inapplicable. The court may decide to override the privilege in the case of a grave or serious crime.

Nevertheless the privilege discussed here is rooted in concern for the patient's right to control access to his personal information. If a child is regarded as mature enough to make conscious decisions in relation to the confidentiality of personal information, then the law should surely recognise this and the child should have the right to make the decision concerning waiver.

In addition, if the child has not yet reached that level of maturity, then there may be situations in which it is necessary for the power of waiver to be entrusted to some other person. This person could be the child's parent or guardian, or it could be the court. The parent is normally the person who makes treatment decisions relating to the child.[39] However, if a dispute arises as to exactly what form of treatment should be given to the child, then the child may be made a ward of court and the decision will then be made by the court. It is suggested that for the purposes of convenience the decision whether to allow waiver should rest in the hands of the court, with the grounds for the decision being the same as in the situation of the deceased patient discussed above.

The gravely ill

Similar considerations apply to the question of waiver and the gravely ill as they do to the child patient. If a person is deprived because of illness of the ability to make choices concerning his future, then that should not mean that others attempting to bring actions on his behalf should be unable to do so. Take, for example, the situation which arose in the tragic case of *Lim Po Chew v Camden Area Health Authority* (1980).[40] In this case a brilliant young Chinese doctor admitted to hospital for an operation suffered brain damage as the result of negligent administration of an anaesthetic. Her relatives brought an action on her behalf, claiming damages against the health authority for the injury suffered. If a medical professional privilege statute had been in force at the time, without some power of waiver, the relatives' action would have been unsustainable. In cases of this type it is submitted that the court should be able to waive the privilege if it is determined that in all the circumstances waiver will be in the best interests of the patient.

WHO IS A DOCTOR FOR THE PURPOSES OF THE PRIVILEGE?

Doctor/psychiatrist

In those jurisdictions where a medical professional privilege statute has been enacted, the relevant statutes invariably provide a definition of what is meant by a 'doctor' for the purposes of the statute. In New York, for example, the Civil Law and Practice Rules for that state refer to licensed physicians.[41] Similarly in Massachusetts the privilege protecting psychotherapist–patient communications defines a psychotherapist as a person licensed to practise medicine who devotes a considerable amount of time to the practice of psychotherapy.[42] I intend to follow a similar approach. Rather than adopting the term 'doctor' or its predecessor 'physician', I prefer to use the words 'medical practitioner'. They describe more accurately the person to whom the patient goes for advice and treatment and accord with the words used in the statute which authorises the office. A fully qualified medical practitioner is one who is registered in the Register of the General Medical Council as provided by the Medical Act 1983. Since I have suggested that the psychiatrist–patient relationship is worthy of special protection, this requires separate definition. Psychiatry is simply a speciality of medicine in very much the same way that general practice is a speciality. A psychiatrist for the purposes of privilege protection is a medical practitioner recognised as a psychiatrist by the Royal College of Psychiatrists.

The quack practitioner

Should a patient be entitled to claim the benefit of privilege protection if the person who they genuinely believe is a registered medical practitioner is revealed to be a charlatan? This may seem far-fetched, but there are examples of it happening. In June 1991 Rakesh Sood was jailed after he had posed as a doctor and had examined pregnant women and authorised abortions.[43] The film *Paper Mask*, which portrayed a hospital porter who takes on the credentials of a trained doctor and who helps run a casualty ward, was based upon a book written by Dr John Collee, who wrote it after working as a locum in a London hospital. Dr Collee was astonished that it was possible for him to arrive and to declare 'I have come to look after casualty' and be allowed to go ahead without any check on his credentials.[44] Margaret Brazier gives an example of a biology teacher who set himself up in practice as a gynaecologist and who remained practising for some considerable time before his eventual detection.[45] Some foreign statutes provide for this contingency. In Illinois, the psychiatrist-patient privilege statute provides that a patient may claim privilege protection for communications made to a psychiatrist who is medically qualified and who devotes a considerable amount of time to the practice of psychiatry or to a person whom the patient 'reasonably believes to be so qualified'.[46] If a patient places his trust in a person who holds himself out to the world at large as being a medical practitioner and on the basis of that representation confides in that person, then there are strong grounds for arguing that the confidentiality of those communications should be protected. To defeat the patient's expectations of confidentiality in the courtroom would amount to imposing an obligation to enquire fully into the medical qualifications of those who treat them. It is suggested that the approach adopted in the State of Illinois should be used as a model and that the privilege should be extended to cover those situations in which the patient reasonably believes that the person who is treating him is medically qualified within the meaning of the statute. Furthermore this reasonable belief should be a test of subjective reasonableness as opposed to objective reasonableness. In most cases objective reasonable belief and subjective reasonable belief that the person is a doctor will coincide. But this is not inevitably so. An example of a situation in which the need for a subjective test is shown is the case of the patient who is perhaps educationally subnormal and who believes quite genuinely that the person who is treating him is a qualified medical practitioner in a situation where on an objective assessment a reasonable person would say that it was quite clear that the person was not qualified.

Psychotherapists

In chapter 4 I discussed the role of the psychotherapist and noted how he will frequently come into the possession of very sensitive confidential information in the course of a therapeutic relationship. But while this relationship may appear at first glance to be ideally suited for privilege protection, in practice there are difficulties in including such therapists within the scope of a privilege statute. These are related to the practice of psychotherapy in this country. At present psychotherapy is practised by a diverse collection of people, medical practitioners, social workers and other counsellors. The United

Kingdom Standing Council is now working towards standardising training and ethical guidelines for psychotherapists.[47] At the present time there are no compulsory licensing requirements, in contrast to the position in the United States, where there are many statutes which regulate psychotherapeutic practice.[48]

In the absence of standardised professional licensing provisions, to include psychotherapists within a privilege statute would be wrong in view of the uncertainty that this could occasion. If standardisation were to occur later, then the position should be reviewed. Those psychotherapists who are medical practitioners will in any event come within the scope of the privilege. The patient will also be able to claim privilege protection if he reasonably believed that the person who treated him was a registered medical practitioner. It is interesting that there is little evidence in this country of patients attempting to stop their therapist giving evidence. In only one case I have come across has there been an attempt by a psychotherapist to claim that he is entitled to refuse to testify. In this case a medical practitioner, one Dr Swan, who had been receiving psychotherapy, was indicted for supplying drugs to addicts.[49] At trial he subpoenaed his analyst, who had refused to give evidence. The judge, very suprisingly, eventually allowed the psychotherapist to refrain from giving testimony after hearing that evidence of character was part of the process of transference of analysis and that he should not be forced to reveal anything about the patient's condition. One further point should be made. If the form of psychotherapy undertaken is psychoanalysis, it is a very lengthy treatment. A patient is usually required to attend consultations on a basis of five consultations per week every week for several years. As a result of this intensity the therapist is able to see only a limited number of patients. Psychotherapy is not available on the National Health Service. The intensity of the treatment and the limited number of patients means that the cost of therapy is heavy, and beyond the reach of most people. Were a privilege to be granted to psychotherapists' patients, this might lead in effect to a class bias between those who could afford the expensive therapy provided by psychotherapists and those who could not. Criticism of such a division has been made in the United States, where it has been suggested that a privilege should be extended to psychiatric social workers who perform therapeutic counselling services for those unable to afford the higher fees of the therapist.[50] If the training requirements and ethical codes for all such counsellors were clearly defined, as it seems that the UKSC for Psychotherapy are trying to achieve, then of course this problem might be overcome. Until those developments occur I suggest that psychotherapists should generally be excluded from privilege protection. If, however, a medical practitioner undertakes psychotherapy, then, since he will be performing what can be described as medical treatment and would otherwise fall under the statute, he should be included within the category of those covered by privilege protection.

Psychologists

Psychologists are trained in the study of human behaviour.[51] They apply their knowledge in many different areas: for example some assist in the development of new products in industry, while others work in the retail trade advising on such matters as the layout of shops and stores. Obviously these are not of concern to us here. In contrast, the work of other psychologists is very much akin to that of the medical practitioner assisting the individual patient with his psychological problems. Clinical psychologists work alongside medical teams in hospitals, and are involved in caring for patients who have problems relating to such things as alcoholism and child abuse. Today they are frequently chartered psychologists having undertaken a postgraduate degree and then obtained the British Psychological Society's Diploma in Clinical Psychology. After qualification they have a well-defined career structure within the National Health Service. Although psychologists, unlike psychiatrists, do not have to qualify as registered medical practitioners in order that they can practise psychology, they are bound by an ethical code. This has been drawn up by the British Psychological Society and provides that:

> Psychologists shall take all reasonable steps to preserve the confidentiality of the information acquired through their professional practice and research and to protect the privacy of individuals and organisations about whom information is collected or held. In general and subject to the requirements of law they shall take care to prevent the identity of individuals, organisations or participants in research being revealed without their express permission.[52]

While the code goes on to provide that in certain situations confidentiality may be broken, these exceptions are very similar to those contained in the codes of ethics of the medical profession.

Psychologists may be involved with information concerning patients which is inherently confidential in its nature. In recognition of this the psychologist–patient privilege has been included within the scope of privilege protection provided in other jurisdictions.[53] The psychologist has become an increasingly familiar figure in the witness box. He may be called to give evidence in the form of relevant data from experiments, or in his actuarial role he can assess the probability of a particular type of behaviour occurring. Clinical psychologists have been called to testify on matters such as whether an individual is capable of handling his own affairs or of whether a defendant is insane.

Psychologists involved in the care and treatment of patients come quite clearly within the criteria suggested in this chapter which should be fulfilled before privilege protection is awarded. It is envisaged that this will mean that initially at least only clinical psychologists will be covered by privilege protection, since it is this branch of psychology which involves the application of knowledge from scientific psychology to treating problems of an emotional and behavioural nature experienced by individual patients.

Dentists

There has been a vast amount of writing in the area of ethical and legal problems in the doctor–patient relationship, but very little in the area of the dentist–patient relationship. There are no reported cases in this country in which a patient has sought to claim privilege for his dental information. There has been a certain degree of privilege protection given to dentist–patient communications in the United States, but this is by no means as comprehensive as the privilege protection given to doctor–patient communications.[54] Nevertheless it should not be forgotten that the dentist–patient relationship is a confidential one. The dental profession in this country, like their medical counterparts, are regulated by a governing body, in this case the General Dental Council. This organisation includes in its code of ethics an obligation to maintain confidentiality to patients. The Code of Conduct of the General Dental Council provides that

> dentists who disclose to a third party, without the patients' permission, information about a patient acquired in a

121

professional capacity, may be considered to have been guilty of an improper breach of confidence. There may, however, be circumstances in which the public interest outweighs the dentist's duty with regard to confidentiality and in which disclosure would be justified.[55]

Dentists are unlikely to obtain as much confidential information about a patient as is obtained about a patient by a general practitioner, for instance. The dentist may obtain a broader range of information than that which simply relates to the patient's dental care since he may need to know of an illness from which the patient is suffering because this may be relevant to the patient's dental treatment.

Dental care is also provided by dental auxiliaries, who perform very minor work in relation to cleaning and polishing teeth. They may provide treatment only under the direction of a registered dentist. Dental auxiliaries are regulated by the General Dental Council, however, and must be enrolled in the Roll of Dental Hygienists or Dental Therapists. They too are bound under their ethical code to preserve confidentiality.

In view of the fact that dentists are professionals and are under a defined obligation to maintain professional confidentiality, it is suggested that were a privilege statute to be enacted, communications between dentist and patient should be subject to privilege protection in the same way as are communications between doctor and patient. It is unlikely that dental auxiliaries would ever be called upon to give evidence relating to a patient's confidential information. Nevertheless in a situation in which dental auxiliaries work under the direction of a registered medical practitioner, a strong argument can be advanced that privilege protection should also cover communications between them and their patients.

Alternative medical practitioners

So far the discussion has concentrated upon those involved in conventional medical practice. But should privilege protection be so limited? Why not extend it to include practitioners of alternative medicine, for instance?[56] By alternative medicine I refer to those areas of treatment such as acupuncture, hypnosis and homoeopathy. There is still much scepticism regarding these forms of treatment. There has been steadfast opposition from practitioners of orthodox medicine to the inclusion of alternative medicine within the area recognised by the

General Medical Council. Despite growing interest and enthusiasm concerning the subject expressed by, amongst others, HRH Prince Charles, this opposition has shown no signs of abating. In 1982, the year in which the Prince was President of the British Medical Association, a working group was set up to explore both the feasibility and possible methods of assessing alternative therapies. The group reported that:

> While we have a duty of fairness to practitioners of alternative therapies our long term duty to our patients is not to support what may be passing fashions but to ensure for them the benefit of medicine in the future. These include future applications of scientific knowledge. But also, and just as important, orthodox medicine carries the safeguards which arise from entrusting the preservation of health and the care of disease to a registered and accountable profession with a long standing tradition of scientific and professional integrity including standards of confidentiality.[57]

Despite the BMA's caution, some doctors have been willing to use alternative therapies. A study in *The Times* as far back as 1974 found that 26 per cent of doctors had tried a form of alternative medicine for their own illness and 57 per cent of doctors who were not practising some kind of alternative therapy said that they would like to do so.[58] A higher proportion of doctors practised some kind of alternative therapy than was previously thought, and a far higher number of medical practitioners than might have been expected referred their patients to alternative medical practitioners. Homoeopathic doctors take a conventional course of medical training before they go on to take a postgraduate course in homoeopathic medicine. The interaction between the two types of practice has been reinforced in one practice in Somerset where NHS and alternative medical practitioners work together in the same building.[59] Various alternative medical associations exist which, while not requiring their members to have some form of conventional medical training, do require some practical and theoretical training, and their members are bound by an ethical code. For example the British Chiropractic Association requires that members of the Association must undergo a four-year full-time course at the Association's only UK college in Bournemouth which leads to a BSc (Chiropractic) degree. Paragraph 5 (a) of the Association's Code of Ethics provides that:

A member shall never betray the confidence of a patient, nor divulge diagnostic findings acquired in the course of professional treatment to anyone without the consent of the patient except where required to do so by law or where failure to do so would constitute a menace or danger to the patient or other member of the community.

It is perhaps premature to include alternative medicine within a privilege statute in this country (although it is interesting to note that communications to chiropractors are privileged in New York[60]). How do we identify who is a practitioner of alternative medicine for the purposes of the privilege? This is a problem we met earlier in relation to the psychotherapist. Unlike the GMC's requirements for the registration of orthodox medical practitioners, there is no standard registration scheme for alternative practitioners.[61] Even if a central register were established, some difficult problems of classification might arise. Take, for example, the Bach flower method. This is based on the healing power of plants, flowers and trees. After diagnosis patients are given remedies of different types of plant oils. The method is aimed at the treatment of emotional states rather than physical ailments. Remedies are given for complaints such as indecision and obsessional thoughts. Despite the fact that the treatment is directed towards emotional disorders, its practitioners rather surprisingly do not see it as a form of psychotherapy, but regard the flower remedies as having physical effects. If a privilege were applied to alternative therapies, which category would this therapy fall under? Is it a form of psychiatric treatment, bearing in mind that psychiatrists frequently use drugs?

At present the chance of such a practitioner being called to give evidence is remote. A recent search of Lexis[62] revealed only sixteen cases which involved alternative medical practitioners. Of these several cases concerned matters in which, even if a privilege had been in existence, the privilege would not have been applicable, such as VAT assessments and planning applications. In none of the other cases was any demur raised about the giving of evidence.

It is submitted that at present such practitioners should be excluded from the ambit of the privilege. But if the present trend continues and the practice becomes more widespread, with practitioners of alternative therapy being subjected to a uniform system of registration as may happen with the advent of the single European market in 1992, then the issue should be reconsidered.

Professions allied to medicine

We saw earlier that it is becoming increasingly common for medical practitioners to work as part of a team involved in the care of the individual patient. While some of the members of that team may be bound by different ethical obligations from those of the medical practitioner, such as the social worker, others, like nurses, have a very similar ethical code. In the United States there has been only limited extension of privilege protection to other professions. This prompts the question, should we include other health professionals within the privilege statute?

The nurse

The nurse is bound by her professional ethical code to preserve the confidentiality of her patients, an obligation similar to that of the registered medical practitioner.[63] Does this obligation lead to the assumption that the patient's right to privacy should be extended to cover communications with the nurse who has been involved in treatment? In the past, this question would have warranted only brief consideration as to whether a nurse acting under the direction of a doctor should come within a privilege. There was little chance that the nurse would be called to testify on the issue of her patient's health. This was the province of the registered medical practitioner. In the past the nurse may have lacked the necessary expertise to testify concerning the patient's progress. Moreover the person with ultimate responsibility for the care of the patient was the doctor under whose direction she would work. In recent years, however, the role of the nurse has steadily expanded:

> Already in the context of hospital nursing and nursing to the community, nurses have been trained to administer drugs intravenously, insert needles into veins for renal dialysis, change tracheotomy tubes, suture superficial wounds, take surgical smears and perform other tasks formerly considered to require a medical practitioner.[64]

The 1986 Cumberlege Report, *Neighbourhood Nursing, A Focus for Care*, recommended that nurses should be given greater responsibilities for making decisions about patients.[65] It proposed the introduction of the 'nurse practitioner', a person who was able to treat patients independently. The nurse practitioner concept was developed in the United States, and although there was considerable opposition to it in the 1970s, it has received increasing support in this country in recent years. The Royal College of Nursing have expressed their agreement with the concept, seeing it as emphasising the nurses' contribution to primary health care. Several nurses have worked as nurse practitioners in this country. Their practice has taken various forms.[66] In one scheme which was set up the nurse orked alongside the doctors in a practice. Patients were given the choice of seeing a doctor or the nurse practitioner. Consultations with the nurse were informal, with nurse and patient sitting at the same table. Patients were encouraged to discuss their problems at length. The nurse in her practice took account of wider issues than the initial symptoms and focused on health education. If needed, the nurse was able to prescribe drugs. The prescription was signed by a doctor who was available at the time. Nurse practitioners have also worked independently. Barbara Burke Masters, for example, worked in a centre for homeless persons with alcohol problems. In effect she acted as a substitute doctor, caring and prescribing for those who came to the centre. Her work – which initially met with great hostility from the medical establishment – filled a void, since general practitioners were unwilling to take homeless persons on to their registers because they would only be registered as temporary residents since they had no fixed address and because of fear of disturbances which such persons might cause at the surgery.

If the role of the nurse continues to expand in the future, situations are likely to arise in which the nurse is the person called upon to give evidence regarding the patient's health. If this were to occur, then the patient who has confided in a nurse should not be in a worse position than that of the patient who has confided in a doctor. The nurse will be acting as a fully autonomous professional. The nurse should thus be included within any medical privilege statute.

Para-medical professionals

Were a privilege statute to be enacted, careful consideration should be given as to whether the para-medical professions should be included.[67] Most of these professions are governed by the Professions Supplementary to Medicine Act 1960. Eight such professions are included under this Act. These are chiropodists, dieticians, occupational therapists, orthoptists, physiotherapists, remedial gymnasts and medical laboratory scientific officers. The Act established a council and eight separate registration boards which cover each of the professions. The council co-ordinates and supervises the activities of the boards and has the task of ensuring that the professions maintain high standards of education, training and professional conduct.

It is a component part of the para-medical practitioners' professional obligation that they preserve patient confidences. But this obligation is less absolute than that owed in certain areas of medical practice such as psychiatry. Para-medical practitioners work alongside medical practitioners or under their direction. As far as at least some of these practitioners are concerned, it appears that their primary duty is owed not to the patient but to the medical practitioner under whose supervision they are working. For example take a statement made in the code of professional conduct of registered radiographers and registered medical laboratory staff. This provides that none of these professionals shall 'knowingly disclose to any patient or to any other unauthorised person the result of any investigation or any other information gained in the practice of his/her profession'. The patient is prohibited along with unauthorised persons from discovering information about his treatment!

The para-medical professional has been recognised in privilege statutes elsewhere. In New Zealand communications with para-medical personnel such as ambulance men are privileged if they are made 'in the course of treatment of any patient by that practitioner'.[68] Some American states have also extended privilege protection to para-medical practitioners. For example Montana includes speech pathologists and audiologists within a privilege, and Ohio protects osteopaths.[69]

Unlike those involved in the practice of alternative medicine, para-medical practitioners are far more easily identifiable because of the definite system of registration which exists. They may be involved in dealing with a patient's confidential information and are generally bound to keep that confidence, but they operate as only part of the general health-care team. They do not owe an obligation to their patient alone.

The code of the Chartered Society of Physiotherapy provides an example of this. Rule 2 of the code provides that

> Chartered physiotherapists shall respect the rights and dignity and individual sensibilities of all their patients.

Similarly Rule 6 provides that

> Chartered physiotherapists shall treat as confidential information obtained by them during the course of their practice of their profession.

This can be contrasted with Rule 4, 'Relationships between the professions':

> Chartered physiotherapists shall communicate and co-operate with other health and allied professions in the interests of the patient.

and also with Rule 5:

> Chartered physiotherapists shall communicate and co-operate with each other and avoid public criticism of colleagues.

If the value of confidentiality is regarded as important for the purposes of the law of evidence, then the confidentiality of the relationship should be scrutinised closely before any privilege is awarded. Without more firm evidence as to the crucially confidential nature of the para-medical practitioner–patient relationship, I would suggest that no privilege should be extended to it.

THE APPLICATION OF THE PRIVILEGE TO TRIBUNAL HEARINGS

The discussion which has taken place so far has been on the basis that the privilege applies in hearings taking place in a court of law. But should a privilege statute be so limited, or should it also extend to tribunals? Tribunals are bodies which were set up as a means by which disputes could be resolved without reference having been made to the ordinary courts of law. They determine issues in many different areas ranging from social security to employment, mental health to taxation. Although application to a tribunal provides a means of challenging an administrative decision, the Franks Committee, who examined the area of tribunals and enquiries, regarded them as part of the machinery of adjudication as opposed to being part of the machinery of administration.[70] Tribunals, they suggested, should be characterised by their openness, fairness and impartiality. Post-Franks, tribunals have become increasingly legalised.[71] In recent years courts of law have been prepared to strike down tribunal decisions on the grounds that the tribunal has not adhered to the rules of procedural fairness. The admission of evidence at many such hearings is a matter left to the discretion of the tribunal chairman. The precise extent to which the rules of evidence apply to tribunal hearings is uncertain. In *W v Egdell*, which was discussed earlier, Scott J held that legal professional privilege did not prevent Dr Egdell's report being adduced at the tribunal hearing.[72] He relied upon two decided cases on the admission of expert evidence. But regrettably his judgment did not address the crucial issue of whether tribunal hearings are legal proceedings to which legal professional privilege applies. The Court of Appeal in that case unfortunately did not pursue that point.

It is instructive to compare the position taken in another common-law jurisdiction, Australia, to the problem of privilege in tribunal hearings. Enid Campbell in her study notes that generally Australian courts have supported the notion that evidential privilege be maintained in tribunal hearings, unless clear statutory words exist expressly removing it.[73] No problem relating to the physician–patient privilege in such hearings appears to have arisen yet.

In the absence of an extensive review of the relationship between the rules of evidence and the tribunal process, the proposals I advance here will necessarily be somewhat tentative. If a patient is, by virtue of his right to privacy, entitled to exclude his confidential medical information from the scrutiny of the court of law, this should also apply to tribunal hearings. Countervailing rights and interests such as the defendant's right to adduce evidence to establish his innocence are less likely to come into conflict with the patient's right to preserve the confidentiality of his medical information at a tribunal hearing than in a court of law on account of the more limited nature of the issues being decided. Similarly tribunals are not concerned with the prosecution of grave crimes. The public interest in encouraging speedy resolution of disputes is of course important, but I suggest that here this interest is outweighed by that of the individual's right to privacy. Moreover, the introduction of the privilege may have little impact in practice. Reports compiled especially for the purpose of the tribunal hearing will not be covered by it, and in many situations it will be in the interest of the person bringing the case to have the information divulged.

There is one type of tribunal hearing from which the privilege statute should, it is suggested, be excluded, however. This is the Mental Health Review Tribunal. The tribunal is empowered to discharge a patient if it finds that the patient is not mentally disordered or that the disorder is not of a nature or degree such as to warrant his detention in hospital or that his detention is not justified in the interests of his own health and safety or that of others.[74] The patient will often request that psychiatric reports be prepared about him for the hearing from independent medical experts and from the responsible hospital authority. The latter is required to submit a report in the form of an account of the patient, his present condition and his suitability for discharge. If a privilege statute were enacted, although a report compiled about the patient would not be privileged since it was not compiled for the purpose of medical treatment, the report from the hospital probably would come within the scope of the privilege, because it would be a report which contained details of the patient's course of treatment for a psychiatric condition. This would deprive the tribunal of anything other than reports compiled by psychiatrists employed by the hospital authorities giving their opinion of the extent of the illness. There would be something extremely artificial in an examination which was made by a hospital psychiatrist for the purposes of the hearing being admitted as evidence if he had been involved in the treatment of the patient previously, whereas the actual records and extracts from his medical history could not be admitted. In assessing the patient's dangerousness to others the tribunal would require details of the previous medical history. It is submitted that the public interest here is such as to justify the privilege being held inadmissible in these hearings. Otherwise the task of the tribunal could be unduly impeded and could possibly lead to the wrong assessment being made, with tragic consequences.

FACTS RELATING TO THE CONSULTATION

If the patient is able to show successfully that his consultation comes within the criteria necessary for him to claim privilege protection, does that also entitle him to claim that the privilege also covers facts relating to the consultation? In the United States, courts in various jurisdictions have decided that facts did not come within the privilege. So, for example, in *Brisenmeister v Supreme Lodge* (1890),[75] the fact that the doctor had attended the insured professionally and the dates and numbers of the consultations were held not to be privileged, and in New York in the case of *Palmer v Supreme Lodge* (1934), while details concerning the diagnosis and treatment of a patient were not admitted as evidence, the dates of entry and discharge and the facts of treatment were held to be admissible.[76]

I would suggest that although generally the fact of a patient's treatment may not be regarded as being of a confidential nature and therefore worthy of inclusion within a privilege statute, there may be certain situations in which the privilege should be extended because the fact of treatment is confidential. A patient who attends a psychiatrist may be sensitive about others knowing not only the details of the consultation, but also the fact that he has been to see a psychiatrist, with the innuendo which might result. This is unlikely to arise in the case of treatment by a GP: most people do not creep surreptitiously to their general practitioner. While patients may be unwilling for the content of their discussion with their practitioner to be disclosed, the fact of the consultation is not by itself confidential in the same way. However, in areas other than psychiatric care the fact of treatment may be very sensitive information. The patient may not want it known that she has been admitted for an abortion or for treatment in a venereal disease clinic. If the facts of the consultation are capable of being regarded as a confidential matter, then they should be included within privilege protection. Facts relating to consultations between psychiatrist and patient should be automatically included within privilege protection. This is in accord with the automatic privilege protection given to the content of such consultations. Facts relating to consultation with other practitioners should only be excluded if they fall within the definition of 'confidential' information protected by the general medical practitioner–patient privilege.

The structure of an evidential privilege statute is, it is hoped, now beginning to emerge. In the final chapter I examine how such a statute would operate in practice, the potential problems it might generate, and to what extent its costs might outweigh its benefits.

6

MEDICAL PRIVILEGE, COSTS AND APPLICATION

MEDICAL CONFIDENTIALITY AND LEGAL PRIVILEGE

The person who goes to his lawyer can feel secure that the information he discloses is confidential even to the extent that it will not be disclosed in subsequent litigation. In contrast, highly sensitive disclosures made by patient to doctor may be divulged in one of the most public fora, the court of law. Should a claim by a patient for privilege of his medical information be granted?

What I have sought to argue in this book is that it is not justifiable to grant a privilege simply on the grounds that doctors, like lawyers, are professionals and that doctors need confidentiality for *their* medical practice. Arguments that medical practice by itself may be hampered by the absence of a privilege are difficult to substantiate. Moreover, to recognise a privilege for medical professionals would be to place them in the unique position in the law of evidence of being able to determine when to disclose the sensitive personal information of others. The privilege given to information between the client and his lawyer is not the lawyer's privilege but that of his client. If we are to enact a privilege for medical confidences, it should be because we believe that the patient has fundamental rights which we need to safeguard. The right to stop disclosure can be seen as part of the patient's right to privacy of personal information.

That in turn does not mean that the patient should be able to veto the disclosure of all information. Rights are not unlimited: the patient's right to privacy is qualified by the countervailing rights of the defendant in a criminal trial to establish his innocence and by various public-policy interests. Futhermore, privacy is a right which is very broad. It encompasses protection of personal information gener-ally. I have suggested that the right to privacy is particularly strong in the context of confidential personal information. The fact that information is labelled 'confidential' should not by itself be enough. Not all medical information meets the criteria of confidentiality, but what does should be protected. Separating the wheat from the chaff, the crucially confidential from the superficially confidential, is no easy task. One way in which this problem might be tackled, I have suggested, is by a distinction being drawn between psychiatric confidentiality and confidentiality as it arises in other areas of medical practice. Information imparted in the psychiatric consultation is generally regarded as crucially confidential. It should therefore be given special protection in the form of a traditional evidential privilege. In contrast the variable position regarding confidential information in the general doctor–patient relationship may be most appropriately reflected by the introduction of an exclusionary discretion.

There is one argument against the introduction of this type of privilege which has not yet been addressed. This is that while a privilege may be justifiable on the basis of protecting important interests, the costs of its introduction are simply too high.

The costs of the privilege

There are certain 'costs' which might result from the introduction of a medical professional privilege. The first is that the legal process might literally cost more. This must surely be a strong argument against any new exclusionary rule of evidence at a time when attempts are being continually made to reduce the cost of the legal process as a whole. The problem with a privilege is that legal proceedings may be prolonged since new issues of law surrounding the admission of medical evidence will be debated. If, for example the medical practitioner–patient privilege were pleaded, the judge would be required to assess whether the communications were 'confidential' in character. Expert evidence may be required, leading to an increase in the number of experts called to give evidence. Litigation is long enough already! There is a danger, however, in exaggerating the potential costs. In many cases there will be no complication because the patient will choose to waive the privilege. Moreover, there is the possibility at the present time that if one party wishes to adduce sensitive medical information, a debate might ensue in the courtroom as to whether or not that evidence should be admitted. Counsel might argue that the judge should use his discretion to exclude evidence. This type of issue may arise more frequently if courts show themselves willing to develop a judicial discretion as shown, for example, in *R v MacDonald*[1]. This will slow down the proceedings. In any case the simple fact that costs may be involved should not deter us from protecting an individual's human rights. An analogy can be drawn with political rights – it may be considerably less expensive to run a nation by means of a dictatorship, but that is not a valid reason for the denial of the individual's right to participate in a democratic election. The proceedings may be speedier without a privilege, but that is not an adequate justification overriding the patient's wish to protect his right of confidentiality.

Another major drawback to introducing medical privilege which can be advanced is that the enactment of a medical professional privilege could result in a domino effect. Other professional groups would campaign for privilege protection on a 'me too' platform. There could be such an extension of professional privilege that, as a consequence, the legal system would be unduly hampered or even break down, with individual cases having to be abandoned because of a lack of sufficient evidence.

One jurisdiction where professional privilege has been accorded on a large scale is the United States. The Revised Uniform Rules of Evidence protect the priest–penitent relationship, this protection being extended in 1974 to cover any confidential communication by a person to a clergyman acting in his capacity as a spiritual advisor.[2] Almost one-third of the states give protection to the accountant-client relationship.[3] Certain states have also granted protection to confidential clerks, stenographers, schoolteachers, counsellors, private detectives and social workers.[4] The parent–child[5] and the subject-researcher relationship have been accorded some privilege protection.[6] There have even been calls in the United States for the extension of privilege to a wide range of intimate relationships on the grounds that this is justified by the need to protect individual privacy. It has been suggested that each person should have twenty to thirty privilege immunities which would cover communications with those individuals with whom he has intimate personal relationships.

Is the flood-gates argument a realistic fear or simply unjustifiable panic? Despite the considerable extension of privilege protection in the United States, there has been no real indication that the American legal system is ready to collapse through a lack of evidence. The extension of privilege protection to cover medical confidences does not mean that we will automatically go on to accord privilege protection to all other relationships because of their confidential nature. In addition the fact that a relationship is 'confidential' in a general sense does not mean that it should be automatically included within the class of relationships formally protected by privilege. While doctors are under a general obligation to keep their patients' secrets, we discovered earlier that, on closer examination, the obligation is variable in different areas of practice. Similarly before the extension of privilege protection to other confidential relationships is contemplated they should, I suggest, be subjected to scrutiny comparable with that undertaken for the doctor–patient relationship. It may be found on closer study that certain relationships, though labelled as 'confidential', lack that quality in any more than a very general rhetorical sense. The feared flood of new privileges may emerge as only a very small trickle.

THE IMPACT OF A PRIVILEGE STATUTE IN PRACTICE

It should not be overlooked that in many cases the enactment of a privilege statute of the type outlined here will have little practical impact because the patient will decide to exercise his right to waive his privilege. The car accident victim who wishes to bring an action claiming negligence to recover damages for the fractured jaw, lacerations and bruises he sustained when the car driven by a drunken driver careered into his own vehicle will be in the same position regardless of the privilege. To establish the extent of damage suffered he will need medical evidence of the extent of the injuries and as to his likely recovery. Even if he is suffering from something such as traumatic neurosis as a result of the accident, evidence of his medical condition will still be given if he decides to waive his privilege because his medical practitioner possesses no veto over the waiver. The privilege is his, not his doctor's.

In a situation in which the patient decides that he will not waive the privilege, a privilege statute will clearly have an impact. It would enable a patient to withhold his sensitive medical information in a court of law and at a tribunal hearing whether he was involved in the case as plaintiff, defendant or witness. But medical evidence may be admitted despite the opposition of the patient because other rights outweigh the patient's privacy right. So, for example, the evidence may be necessary to establish the innocence of a defendant in a

135

criminal trial, or may be required for the prosecution of a grave crime or in a case relating to the care or custody of a child. Not only will the psychiatrist to whom a psychopath confides information about a murder which he has committed be protected under his ethical code if he discloses that fact to the police on the grounds that he was acting in the public interest, but the facts disclosed would very probably be admissible as evidence. The prosecution involves an extremely serious offence, and it is almost certain that admission of the evidence would cause a jury to take a different view of the evidence from the one they would have taken had the questions not been allowed. However, particular problems may arise from the use of the privilege statute in practice.

The impact of third-party involvement

Where two people undergo treatment together and then later one of them wants disclosure in court, what would be the impact of a privilege statute? This situation is most likely to arise in the context of psychiatry, psychotherapy and psychosexual counselling. An example introduced in an earlier chapter may be helpful here. A husband and wife receive psychosexual counselling from their GP. Later the husband is charged along with a co-accused of the rape of a young girl. He wants to put forward evidence of his lack of propensity to commit the offence. As evidence to support his claim he wants to call the GP to testify as to his observations of him during the therapy session. Husband and wife are now living apart, their marriage having broken down. The wife objects strongly to details of the therapy being disclosed in court. Prior to a privilege statute being enacted this evidence would be admissible. Would a privilege make any difference? The husband would probably claim that he was entitled to waive his privilege. The wife would allege that he could not do this because the privilege was just as much hers as his. It is likely that a judge would hold that the information had the necessary quality of confidence, psychosexual counselling being a highly sensitive matter. The husband could argue and would probably succeed in his claim that without the evidence the jury would probably take a different view of his innocence. In addition the public-policy exception to the privilege on the ground that the offence which was being tried was indictable would probably also lead the judge to decide to override the privilege.

A direct clash of interests between the interests of the individual in keeping the confidentiality of his medical information and that of the party bringing an action in a court of law may cause difficulties in a matrimonial dispute.

The nullity dilemma

If a marriage breaks up, then the parties have several options. They may apply for an order of judicial separation, or one or other of the parties may petition the courts for a decree that the marriage is a nullity or for a decree of divorce. It is in the latter two situations that medical evidence may be relevant. One of the grounds upon which a party may petition for divorce is that of unreasonable behaviour. A claim of unreasonable behaviour is frequently connected to the mental condition of the spouse. In *Katz v Katz* (1972),[7] for example, the husband was a manic depressive who had spent some time in a mental hospital. He continually demeaned the wife before visitors and called her a slut before the children. In this type of case a wife petitioning for divorce on the grounds of her husband's unreasonable behaviour would want to call her husband's GP and psychiatrist, and possibly those involved in treating him in a mental hospital, to give evidence.

Similarly medical evidence would be of vital importance in proceedings such as those of *Thurlow v Thurlow* (1975).[8] The wife in this case suffered from a mental disorder which deteriorated and resulted in her being less able to perform her domestic duties. She started to behave erratically, threw articles at her mother-in-law, who lived with them, burnt items on the electric heater, started to wander aimlessly about the streets and eventually was admitted to hospital with no prospect of recovery. Her husband petitioned for divorce on the ground of unreasonable behaviour. In determining this issue medical evidence as to her condition is of vital importance.

If a privilege statute were enacted, it is possible that the medical evidence of the husband in the first example and the wife in the second would be privileged. But without this evidence being admitted, attempts at litigation by the respective spouses of those individuals would be exceedingly difficult.

There is one way in which such a direct conflict of interests between the parties could be overcome, and that is by ordering a medical report to be prepared about the party whose health was the subject of dispute. Such a report would not be privileged since it would have not been compiled for the purposes of medical treatment. It would also have the effect of avoiding the conflict which might also occur if both spouses, one of whom was now petitioning for divorce, had at some time previously attended psychosexual counselling and then later one of them wanted to adduce evidence of the counselling session while the other resisted the production of the evidence.

An even more difficult situation arises in the situation in which one of the parties wishes to petition for a decree of nullity. Two of the grounds upon which a court may make a decree of nullity are that at the time of the marriage ceremony either party was suffering from a mental disorder of such a type or extent that the sufferer was unfitted for marriage or that at the time of the ceremony the respondent was suffering from venereal disease in a communicable form. For the petitioner to establish those facts it would be necessary for the medical records of the respondent which are contemporaneous with the marriage ceremony to be produced. If the respondent did not consent to the production of the records then difficulties would arise, since the statute which I have advocated in the preceding chapter would *prima facie* stop the disclosure of such information, since medical records relating to mental disorder would come under the blanket privilege protection and evidence of venereal disease would surely be classed as confidential information for the purposes of the general practitioner–patient relationship. The petitioner might, of course, still seek a decree of divorce as an alternative, but this might be an unrealistic solution if he belonged to a religious denomination which does not recognise divorce, such as the Church of England. This is a 'hard case'.

Curiously there is little evidence in other jurisdictions of this causing a problem. In one of the few cases in which the use of medical privilege in an annulment action was challenged in New York State, *Jones v Jones* (1955),[9] a privilege was asserted to stop an obstetrician from giving testimony in a case involving an allegation that the wife was at the time of the wedding two months pregnant by another. The very general reviews conducted by law reform bodies into the feasibility or otherwise of the enactment of a medical-privilege statute are of no use to us here. Although foreign law-reform bodies have addressed themselves to general principles on which legislation has been based, they have not considered many of the practical difficulties which their privilege may occasion in any great detail. I hesitate to prefer a solution to this problem. On the one hand we have the problem that should privilege apply here, we may be inhibiting a cause of action totally. On the other hand, to allow disclosure will mean overriding the right of the patient to confidentiality. The drawback with the balancing of conflicting rights is starkly revealed.

Tentatively I suggest that as far as nullity proceedings are concerned, the privilege should be held to be inapplicable.

The employee and his medical records

Medical evidence may often be of great importance in employment law cases, particularly in the area of unfair dismissal. The law on unfair dismissal is purely statutory and is contained in the Employment Protection (Consolidation) Act 1978. The legislation entitles an employee who claims that he has been dismissed unreasonably to bring his case to an industrial tribunal.[10]

One ground for dismissal is that the employee lacked the necessary capacity to perform the job he was employed to do. Medical evidence may be required at two stages in an unfair dismissal case. The first stage arises if the employer claims that he has not dismissed the employee, but his employee has instead left his job. The employee, in order to bring an action, will need to show that he has been dismissed or has resigned in circumstances which amounted to constructive dismissal.[11] The employer may counter this by claiming that the contract has been 'frustrated' because the employee's illness made him unable to perform his job and therefore the contract had been brought to an end.[12] In determining frustration an industrial tribunal will take into account issues such as the nature of the illness. If the illness is of a serious nature, then the employee may be unable to resume work for a very considerable period of time. The employer will argue that his production will be hindered without an employee fulfilling that role.

At first glance it might seem that an employee could sabotage a claim of frustration by use of medical professional privilege. In practice, however, this is unlikely. The employer will probably have taken steps to discover the precise nature and extent of his employee's illness before he informed the employee that his job was no longer available. Any medical report compiled would be admissible because it would not be part of the patient's treatment.

The second stage when medical evidence may be important arises once the employee has shown that he has been dismissed. Under the employment legislation the employer then has the burden of proof of showing that the reason for his dismissal was lawful because it came within one of the grounds for dismissal provided in the 1978 Act and the dismissal was 'reasonable'.[13] An employee can be dismissed if he lacks the 'capability' to perform the job. Section 57 (7) of the

Employment Act 1978 provides that this is to be assessed by reference to skill, aptitude, health or any other relevant physical or mental quality. The employer may argue that he was right to dismiss because his employee's illness made him incapable of work. However, the existence of privilege here also is unlikely to prove fatal to the employer's case. In the case of *Lynoch v Cereal Packaging* (1988),[14] Wood J noted that the employer was not bound to obtain a medical report before he dismissed the employee:

> Where unconnected periods or intermittent periods of absence are concerned, it is impossible to give a reasonable projection of the possibility of what may happen in the future. Whilst an employer may make such enquiries there is no obligation upon him to do so because the results may prove to be of no assistance to him. Nor is there any principle that the mere fact that the employee is fit at the time of the dismissal makes the dismissal unfair.[15]

This case concerned persistent intermittent absence by the employee. It has been suggested that, despite the fact that there is no legal requirement to get such a report, the employer may be wise to obtain one on the grounds that there may be a serious underlying condition which is the reason for these absences.

At the final stage of deciding whether the employer acted reasonably the tribunal will take into account factors similar to those used in determining frustration, including the nature of the illness and the length of absence. The employer should consult with his employee before dismissal.[16] In practice it is likely that the employer will have asked the employee to submit himself to a medical examination by the firm's doctor or alternatively will have asked him if he can get information about his health and likely prognosis from his family doctor. If the employer took steps such as these, the tribunal would be prepared to find that he had acted reasonably.

It seems, then, that although a medical professional privilege statute may have the effect of debarring direct access to the employee's medical records, the employer will already have information concerning the employee's medical condition, information which will not come within the statutory definition of 'confidential' after it has been disclosed to the firm. In practice, therefore, the statute is unlikely to have much real impact in this type of case.

CONCLUSION

When Warren and Brandeis wrote at the end of the last century of the need to safeguard the privacy of the individual, they were writing at a time of an increasingly powerful press and of slow encroachment upon the ability of the individual to live his life free from the scrutiny of others. The considerations which motivated their writings, then, are even more pertinent today, when, through wider means of surveillance by public and private bodies, the individual attempting to keep something of himself private faces an increasingly difficult task. The law, as we have seen, is gradually affording greater recognition to individual privacy rights while stopping short of enacting a privacy statute.

The conclusions of this book will not be received with any sympathy by those who strongly advocate the total abolition of all evidential privileges on the grounds that the number of exclusionary rules in the law of evidence should be very small. One of the earliest advocates of this approach, Jeremy Bentham, believed that there should be as little impediment to the fact-finding process as possible and that evidence should be only excluded if it came within one of a limited number of categories.[17] More recently the Law Reform Committee[18] noted that it was the policy of the common law to limit to a minimum the categories of privilege which a person had a right to claim. A general reduction in the number of situations in which evidence may be excluded in English law has come about in recent years, a good example being provided by the hearsay rule.[19] Unlike many other exclusionary rules which are justified on the basis that the tribunal of fact is not faced with unreliable evidence, privilege rules exclude evidence because of some perceived interest and individual right – the right of litigants to obtain legal advice in order that they can effectively propound their case, for example, or the public interest in military secrets being kept.

Galligan has written that:

the criminal trial and the rules of evidence which regulate it can be understood in different ways. The first puts overriding emphasis on rectitude. The second modifies that emphasis by introducing the notion of a right to a fair trial and the matching idea that the trial must be tipped in favour of not convicting the innocent even at the cost of increasing the risk of acquitting the guilty. The third approach goes beyond the second by allowing that probative evidence might be lost or withheld from the trial process in order to serve values independently of outcome.[20]

Despite the stress placed upon the need for all relevant evidence to be placed before the court, the English law of evidence already resembles the third of Galligan's three alternatives. Rules of evidence do exist which have the effect of safeguarding values unrelated to rectitude of outcome. The public-policy exclusionary rule provides one of the best examples of this, and section 78 of the Police and Criminal Evidence Act 1984 is another such example. A medical privilege would not therefore be a complete aberration. Moreover, while a privilege may have the effect of excluding relevant and reliable evidence, if an interest can be identified as important enough, the law should not hesitate to afford it protection. It is submitted that the patient's interest in ensuring that the doctor keeps his confidences entrusted in him is such an interest.

This book has been solely concerned with medical privilege, but it remains a live issue whether, if confidentiality and privacy rights are important, these should be recognised in the law of evidence as a whole. There is need for scrutiny of the many statutes which at present require disclosure of evidence to see to what extent they are really necessary. In addition we should perhaps consider whether other relationships need protection in the courtroom as in other jurisdictions. Recently, much time has been spent upon drafting a criminal code. Perhaps it is time for a written code of evidence to be promulgated in this country and for the questions of countervailing rights in the context of the law of evidence to be aired publicly.

NOTES

1 SHOULD THE DOCTOR TELL?

1 See F. Gurry, *Breach of Confidence* (1984) and discussion later in this chapter about the expansion of the law of breach of confidence.
2 Data Protection Act 1984, Access to Personal Files Act 1987 and Access to Health Records Act 1990.
3 See the discussion in chapter 3 below.
4 *X v Y* [1988] 2 All ER 648.
5 See *Duchess of Kingston's Case* (1776) 20 State Trials 355 and chapter 2 below.
6 *D v NSPCC* [1978] AC 171.
7 See further *Rogers v Secretary of State for the Home Department* [1973] AC 388, Contempt of Court Act 1981, s. 10 and further discussion of these issues in chapter 2 below.
8 Cited in *Prince Albert v Strange* (1849) 1 Mac and G 25, 1 H & TW 1, Court of Chancery.
9 Law Commission Report No. 110, *Breach of Confidence* (1981) Cmnd 8388, p. 10.
10 [1967] Ch D 102.
11 [1988] 2 WLR 1280.
12 See note 4 *supra*.
13 [1969] 1 QB 349.
14 *Ibid.*, p. 362.
15 [1984] 2 All ER 417.
16 *Ibid.*, p. 422.
17 See note 4 *supra*, p. 650.
18 [1989] 1 All ER 1085 and in the Court of Appeal [1990] 2 WLR 471. See the discussion of this case and the question of medical confidentiality by M. Jones, 'Medical Confidentiality and the Public Interest' (1990) *Professional Negligence* 16.
19 [1990] 2 WLR 493.
20 Case reported in the *Guardian Law Reports*, 8 May 1990.
21 See, for example, P. Mathews, 'Legal Privilege and Breach of Confidence', 1:1 *Legal Studies* 77 and N. H. Andrews, 'The Influence of Equity upon the Doctrine of Legal Professional Privilege' (1989) 105 *LQR* 608.
22 [1987] QB 670.

23 *Ibid.*, p. 608.

2 COMPARISONS AND INCONSISTENCIES

1 C. Tapper, *Cross on Evidence*, 7th edn (London, 1990), p. 416.
2 (1776) 20 State Trials 355.
3 (1881) 17 Ch D 675.
4 *Ibid.*, p. 681.
5 (1920) TLR 196.
6 (1964) 108 *Sol J* 605.
7 [1974] QB 767.
8 *Ibid.*, p. 775.
9 Criminal Law Revision Committee, Eleventh Report, *Evidence (General)* (1972) Cmnd 4991, para. 274, pp. 158-9.
10 See pp. 27 below.
11 *D v NSPCC* [1978] AC 171.
12 Section 10, Contempt of Court Act 1981.
13 See further Tapper, op. cit.
14 [1886] 2 Ch D 644.
15 *Ibid.*, p. 648.
16 (1833) 1 My & K 98.
17 [1930] AC 558, p. 568.
18 [1988] 2 All ER 246.
19 [1980] AC 524.
20 *Ventouris v Mountain* [1991] 1WLR 607.
21 *R v Barton* [1972] 2 All ER 1192 , Caulfield LJ, p. 1193.
22 (1884) 14 QBD 153.
23 [1942] AC 524.
24 *Rogers v Secretary of State for the Home Department* [1973] AC 388.
25 [1978] AC 171.
26 *Ibid.*, p. 190.
27 *Ibid.*, p. 220.
28 *Ibid.*, p. 218.
29 *Ibid.*, p. 230.
30 [1988] 2 All ER 648.
31 *Ibid.*, p. 661.
32 See, for example, *Gaskin v Liverpool City Council* [1980] 1 WLR 1549 and *Science Research Council v Nasse* [1980] AC 1028.
33 16 January 1991, transcript on Lexis.
34 See, for example, the dictum of Megarry VC in *Malone v MPC* [1979] 2 All ER 620, p. 642:

It is no function of the courts to legislate in a new field.The extension of existing laws and principles is one thing. The creation of an altogether different right, another. At times judges must, and do, legislate; but as Holmes J once said, they do so intentionally and with molecular rather than molar motions.

35 See further Lord Edmund Davies in *Waugh v BRB* [1980] AC 521, p. 543.

36 See the discussion by G. Noakes, 'Professional Privilege' [1950] 66 *LQR* 94.
37 (1828) 3 C & P 518.
38 (1853) 6 Cox CC 219.
39 Tapper, op. cit., p. 447.
40 See note 30 *supra*, p. 98.
41 [1981] AC 1096.
42 *Secretary of State for Defence v Guardian Newspapers* [1984] 3 All ER 601.
43 [1988] 2 WLR 33.
44 [1990] 2 WLR 1000.
45 *Ibid.*, 1019.
46 J. H. Wigmore, *A Treatise on the Anglo-American System of Evidence in Trials at Common Law*, 3rd edn, Vol. 8 (Toronto, 1983), p. 818.
47 Advisory Committee, *Note to Proposed Federal Rule of Evidence 504*, 36 FRD 183, 4241-2 42 (1972). Though note its development via Federal Rule of Evidence 501: see further C. M. Bernstein, 'The Psychotherapist-Patient Privilege under Federal Rule of Evidence 501' (1984) 1 *Journal of Criminal Law and Criminology* 388.
48 See J. Beigler, 'Psychiatric Confidentiality and the American Legal System', in S. Bloch and P. Chodoff, *Psychiatric Ethics*, 2nd edn (Oxford, 1991).
49 28 USCS Appendix, Federal Rules of Evidence, Rule 504, appendix 6.
50 See 'Psychotherapist-Patient Privilege', 72 *ALR Fed* 395, p. 399.
51 See generally 'Developments in Privileged Communications', 98 *Harv LR* 1450.
52 Code of Civil Procedure stat Quebec 1969 c. 80, Medical Act s.40, stat Quebec 1973 c. 46.
53 Quebec Code of Civil Procedure 1965 (Queb) c. 80 s. 308.
54 (1963) 21 RFL 46.
55 (1970) DLR (3a) 168 ONLR.
56 (1970) 11 DLR (3d) 673, 689-90.
57 *Ibid.*, 673.
58 (1978) 39 CCC (2d) 226 (Ont CA). See also *R v Burgess* [1974] 4 WWR 310.
59 *Ibid.*, at p. 230.
60 See Evidence 12, *Professional Privileges before the Court*.
61 Federal Provincial Task Force on the Uniform Rules of Evidence, ch. 32, 'Professional Privileges'.
62 (1975) 55 DLR (3d).
63 Evidence Act 1910, s. 96 (2) (Tasmania); Evidence Ordinance 1939-1972, s. 18 (2) (Northern Territory); Evidence Act 1958, s. 28 (2) (Victoria). See further D. Byrne and J. D. Heydon, *Cross on Evidence*, 3rd Australian edn (1986), pp. 625-54 and G. L. Peirris, 'Medical Professional Privilege' in (1984) 33 *Int and Comparative LQ* 301.
64 Australian Law Reform Commission Report No. 38, *Evidence*, ch. 32, 'Professional Privilege'.
65 Evidence Act (NZ) 1908, s. 8.
66 [1963] 2 QB 447.

67 *Ibid.*, p. 489.
68 Law Reform Committee, Sixteenth Report, *Law of Evidence in Civil Proceedings* (1967) Cmnd 3472.
69 See note 9 *supra*.
70 [1978] AC 191, p. 227.
71 *Ibid.*, p. 239.
72 *Ibid.*, p. 243, and see also the discussion in R. D. Pattenden, *The Judge, the Discretion and the Criminal Trial* (Oxford, 1987), pp. 117–19.
73 See note 33 *supra*.
74 [1980] AC 402.
75 See Lord Diplock, pp. 436–7; Lord Fraser, p. 449; Lord Scarman, p. 456; Viscount Dilhorne, p. 411; Lord Salmon, p. 445.
76 *R v Payne* (1963) 47 Cr App R 122.
77 [1980] AC 402, p. 440.
78 [1991] *Crim LR* 122.
79 See St John Robillard and J. McEwan, *Police Powers and the Individual* (Oxford, 1986), p. 224.
80 [1913] AC 417. See also the Law Commission Report (1966) Cmnd 3149, *Report upon the Powers of Appeal Courts to sit in Private and upon Publicity in Domestic Proceedings*.
81 *In Re Farber* 78 NJ 259, 274–81, 394 A 2d 370 Cert denied 439 US 997 (1978).
82 P. Westen, 'Compulsory Process II' (1975) 74 *Mich LR* 192, p. 248, note 198.
83 A. Hill, 'Testimonial Privilege' (1980) *Columbia LR* 1173.
84 *Ibid.*, p. 1186.

3 CONFIDENTIALITY: A PRINCIPLE TO BE PROTECTED?

1 J. Bentham, *Introduction to the Principles of Morals and Legislation*, ed. J. H. Burns and H. L. A. Hart (London, 1980).
2 For further discussion concerning act utilitarianism and rule utilitarianism see A. Quinton, *Utilitarian Ethics* (London, 1973).
3 J. S. Mill, *Utilitarianism*, first published 1879; this edition 1791.
4 *Ibid.*, p. 257.
5 Ormston, 'The Interpretation of the Moral Philosophy of J. S. Mill', in P. Foot, *Theories of Ethics* (Oxford, 1967).
6 J. J. C. Smart, 'Extreme and Restricted Utilitarianism', in Foot, op. cit.
7 See Quinton, op. cit.
8 J. D. Mabbott, 'Interpretations of Mill's Utilitarianism', reprinted in Foot, op. cit.
9 J. Bentham, *Rationale of Judicial Evidence*, first published 1825, reprinted 1981.
10 W. Twining, *Theories of Evidence: Bentham and Wigmore* (London, 1985).
11 *Ibid.*

12 J. H. Wigmore, *A Treatise on the Anglo-American System of Evidence in Trials at Common Law*, 3rd edn (Boston, Mass., 1940).

13 *Ibid.*, p. 2285.

14 D. Fisher, 'The Psychotherapeutic Profession and the Law of Privileged Communications', 10 *Wayne LR* 5609.

15 *Ibid.*, p. 5646.

16 Wigmore, op. cit., p. 2380a.

17 Z. Chafee Jr, 'Is Justice Served or Obstructed by Closing the Doctor's Mouth on the Witness Stand?', 52 *Yale LJ* 607.

18 D. W. Shuman, W. F. Weiner and G. I. Pinnard, 'The Privilege Study' (1986) 9 *International Journal of Law and Psychiatry* 393.

19 See Wigmore, op. cit.

20 G. E. Moore, *Principia Ethica*, first published 1903; reprinted Harmondsworth, 1985.

21 J. J. C. Smart and B. Williams, *Utilitarianism: For and Against* (Cambridge, 1985).

22 R. Tuck, *Natural Rights Theories: Their History and Development.* (Cambridge, 1981).

23 W. Hohfeld, *Fundamental Legal Conceptions* (New Haven, Conn., 1923).

24 French Code, Penal Article 378.

25 M. Cranston, *What Are Human Rights?* (London, 1973).

26 M. MacDonald, 'Natural Rights', in J. Waldron, *Theories of Rights* (Oxford, 1982).

27 J. Bentham, *Anarchical Fallacies*, the full text of which is included along with commentary in J. Waldron (ed.), *Nonsense on Stilts: Bentham, Burke and the Rights of Man* (London, 1987).

28 H. L. A. Hart, *Essays on Bentham, Jurisprudence and Political Theory*, (Oxford, 1982), ch. IV, 'Natural Rights, Bentham and J. S. Mill'.

29 See the full text of E. Burke, 'Reflection on the Revolution in France', cited in Waldron, op. cit.

30 See further the discussion by T. Campbell in *The Left and Rights* (London, 1983).

31 The United Nations Declaration was adopted by the General Assembly of the United Nations on 10 December 1948; the European Convention of Human Rights was drafted in 1950 and entered into force on 3 September 1953.

32 J. Finnis, *Natural Law and Natural Rights* (Oxford, 1984).

33 C. Henkin, 'Rights Here and There', 81 *Columbia LR* 1600.

34 T. Hobbes, *Leviathan* (London, 1651).

35 J. Locke, *Two Treatises of Government* (London, 1689).

36 Adopted on 4 July 1776.

37 See Cranston, op. cit.

38 The United Kingdom made a declaration under Article 25 of the Convention accepting the right of individuals to petition against it. The first of such declarations was made by the United Kingdom on 14 January 1966.

39 J. S. Mill, *On Liberty*, first published 1859; reprinted Oxford, 1985.

40 See the introduction to the 1985 reprint of *On Liberty* by Gertrude Himmelfarb.

41 (1890) *Harv LR* 193.
42 L. J. Paper, *Brandeis* (1982), see p. 32.
43 See Warren and Brandeis, op. cit., p. 195.
44 277 US 438, 48 S. Ct 564 (1928).
45 A. Westin, *Privacy and Freedom* (New York, 1969).
46 C. Fried in F. D. Schoeman, *Philosophical Dimensions of Privacy: An Anthology* (Cambridge, 1984).
47 W. Parent, 'The Right to Privacy' (1983) 2 *Law and Philosophy* 305.
48 C. Henkin, 'Privacy and Autonomy' (1974) *Columbia LR* 1742.
49 See, for example, *Roe v Wade* 410 US 133 (1973).
50 See further 'Developments Privileged Communications', 98 *Harv LR* 1450.
51 A. Ashworth, 'Excluding Evidence as Protecting Rights' (1977) *Crim LR* 723.
52 D. Galligan, 'The Right to Silence Reconsidered' (1988) *CLP* 69.
53 I. Dennis, 'Corroboration Requirements Reconsidered' (1984) *CLP* 316.
54 See Galligan, op. cit., p. 32.
55 See Wigmore, op. cit., p. 51.
56 St. Eliz C. 9 512.
57 Wigmore, op. cit., p. 51.
58 *Countess of Shrewsbury's Trial* 2 Hour St T 768.
59 (1890) 25 QBD 494 CA.
60 [1972] 2 All ER 1192.
61 *Ibid.*, p. 1192.
62 [1968] AC 910.
63 *Ibid.*, p. 941.
64 *R v Lewis JJ ex parte Home Secretary* [1973] AC 388, p. 407.
65 T. R. S. Allan, 'Legal Privilege and the Accused – An Unfair Balancing Act' [1989] 138 *NLJ* 688.
66 [1988] AC 388, p. 407.
67 [1991] *Crim LR* 533.
68 J. C. Smith, 'Comment' [1991] *Crim LR* 535.
69 See further A. Hill, 'Testimonial Privilege and a Fair Trial', 80 *Columbia LR* 1173, and D. M. Paccicco, 'The Constitutional Right to Present Defence Evidence in Criminal Cases' (1989) *Can Bar Review* 518.
70 *In Re Farber* 78 NJ, 259, 394 A 2d 370.
71 See Hill, op. cit., p. 1175.
72 [1965] AC 595
73 [1951] 2 KB 600.
74 (1981) 76 Cr App R 271.
75 [1974] AC 85 PC.
76 [1975] QB 834.
77 *Ibid.*, p. 842.
78 (1986) 72 Cr App R 78.
79 *R v McMillan* (1979) 29, CRNS 798, quoted in (1986) *Crim LR* 92.
80 [1884] 14 QBD 153.
81 [1895] 2 Ch D 751.

82 *Ibid.*, p. 755.
83 [1975] 3 All ER 446.
84 (1985) 82 Cr App R 295 CA.
85 The following states expressly limit the privilege to civil cases: California, Montana, Oregon and Utah.
86 74 Idaho 258 p 2d 571 (1953).
87 101 Cal 513 3d p 16 (1893).
88 P. Bromley, *Family Law*, 8th edn (London, 1992), p. 38.
89 409 Mis 2d 969 42244 NYS 2d 441 (1963).
90 108 NJ 149, 260 (1969).
91 30 Dist Cal Ap 294 168 Cal Rep 558.
92 S. 32 Criminal Justice Act 1988.
93 See further the discussion in J. Spencer and R. Flinn, *The Evidence of Children* (London, 1990).
94 [1970] 1 WLR 599.
95 I. Dennis, 'Reconstructing the Law of Criminal Evidence' (1989) *CLP* 42.
96 *Ibid.*, p. 30.
97 Report of the Committee on Privacy (1972) Cmnd 5012.

4 CONFIDENTIALITY: RHETORIC OR REALITY?

1 British Medical Association, *Philosophy and Practice of Medical Ethics* (London, 1987) and General Medical Council, Blue Book, *Professional Conduct and Fitness to Practise* (1985).
2 M. Phillips and J. Dawson, *Doctor's Dilemmas* (Brighton, 1984).
3 J. K. Mason and R. A. McCall Smith, *Law and Medical Ethics*, 3rd edn (London, 1991).
4 S. Lock and I. Loudan, 'A Question of Confidentiality', *BMJ* 288 (1984), 123, 125.
5 J. H. Wigmore, *A Treatise on the Anglo-American System of Evidence*, 3rd edn, Vol. 8 (Toronto, 1983), p. 823.
6 A. Miles, *The Mentally Ill in Contemporary Society*, 2nd edn (New York, 1987).
7 *Taylor v US* 95 US App DC 373 322 FD 398 at 402 (1955), quoting from Guttmacher and Weihofen, *Psychiatry and the Law* (1952), p. 272.
8 See further J. Holmes and R. Lindley, *The Value of Psychotherapy* (Oxford, 1989).
9 See paragraph 2 of the Constitution of the United Kingdom Standing Conference for Psychotherapy.
10 See further J. Fry, *Present State and Future Needs in General Practice* (London, Royal College of General Practitioners, 1983).
11 See chapter 5 below.
12 J. Huntington, *Social Work and General Practice: Collaboration or Conflict?* (London, 1981).
13 H. W. S Francis, 'Of Gossips, Eavesdroppers and Peeping Toms' *Journal of Medical Ethics* 8 (1982), 134.
14 I. Thompson, 'The Nature of Confidentiality', *Journal of Medical Ethics* 5 (1979) and P. Sieghart, 'Professional Ethics, for Whose Benefit?', *Journal of Medical Ethics* 8 (1982), 25.

15 M. R. Brazier, *Medicine, Patients and the Law* (London, 1992), p. 57.
16 M. Siegler, 'Medical Confidentiality – A Decrepit Concept', *New England Journal of Medicine* 307 (1982), 1518.
17 See further 'Ethics in Nursing: The Caring Relationship', ch. 10 in V. Tschudin, *Ethical Issues in Nursing Practice* 2nd edn (London, 1992).
18 *Code of Professional Conduct for the Nurse, Midwife and Health Visitor* (London, UKCC for Nursing, Midwifery and Health Visitors, 1992).
19 D. Black and F. Subotsky, 'Medical Ethics and Child Psychiatry', *Journal of Medical Ethics* 8 (1982), 5.
20 See further *X v Y* [1988] 2 All ER 648. Infertility treatment is regarded as being of such social sensitivity that when legislation was passed to regulate this treatment a statutory ban was placed upon disclosure of information concerning those receiving treatment; see Human Fertilisation and Embryology Act 1990, s. 33.
21 See further D. Kloss, *Occupational Health* (London, 1989).
22 *Ibid.*, p. 57.
23 Cited in G. Howard, 'OH Managers and Employee Legislation', *Occupational Health* (1988), 670.
24 See anonymous letter, *Journal of Medical Ethics* 8 (1982), 213.
25 P. Bowden, 'Medical Practice, Defendants and Prisoners', *Journal of Medical Ethics* 2 (1976), 163.
26 See further report of the Advisory Council on the Misuse of Drugs, *Aids and Drug Misuse Part I*, (London, HMSO, 1989).
27 *Prison Disturbances April 1990, Report of an Inquiry by the Rt Hon Lord Justice Woolf and His Honour Judge Stephen Tumin* (London, HMSO, 1990), Cmnd 1456, para 12.370.
28 S. Shaw, 'HIV and AIDS', *Am BoV Quarterly* 37 (April 1990), 7, discussing the position in Edinburgh prison, noted that 'I was also struck by the fact that medical confidentiality seemed to be fully respected . . . in Saughton it was appreciated that "need to know" was a nonsense.'
29 See Mason and McCall Smith, op. cit., p. 123.
30 Francis, op. cit., p. 143.
31 R. Gillon, 'AIDS and Medical Confidentiality', *BMJ* 294 (1987), 1675.
32 *Ibid.*
33 See Mason and McCall Smith, op. cit., p. 143.
34 Brazier, op. cit., p. 37.
35 See further M. Rosenbaum, 'Children's Rights', in P. Sieghart, *Human Rights in the United Kingdom* (London, 1988).
36 *Gillick v West Norfolk and Wisbech AHA* [1986] AC 150.
37 *Ibid.*, p. 188.
38 Brazier, op. cit., p. 339.
39 J. Montgomery, 'Confidentiality and the Immature Minor' (1987) *Family Law* 101.
40 [1966] 2 QB 414.
41 *Ibid.*, p. 419.
42 Public Health (Control of Disease) Act 1984 and Public Health (Infectious Diseases) Regulations 1968 (SI 1968 No. 1366).

43 Abortion Act 1967, s.2 (Abortion Regulations SI 1968 No. 390) (as amended). Information concerning a person's infertility treatment which is protected from disclosure by s. 33 of the Human Fertilisation and Embryology Act 1990 may be disclosed in certain circumstances. For example, the clinician at the infertility clinic may disclose patient information to the patient's solicitor where this is necessary for the purpose of bringing legal proceedings (see Human Fertilisation and Embryology Act 1990, s. 33(6f) (as amended)) or where it is necessary to avert imminent danger to the health of the patient (see *ibid.*, s. 33(6e) (as amended)) and it is not reasonably possible to get the patient's consent.

44 Road Traffic Act 1988, s. 172.

45 Prevention of Terrorism (Temporary Provisions) Act 1989, s. 18.

46 Police and Criminal Evidence Act 1984, s. 9 and s. 11 Schedule I.

47 This has been strongly advocated by A. A. S. Zuckerman, 'The Weakness of the PACE Special Procedure for Protecting Confidential Material' (1990) *Crim LR* 472.

48 P. Schutte, 'Medical Confidentiality and a Police Murder Inquiry', *Journal of the Medical Defence Union* (1989), 21.

49 See Brazier, op. cit., Mason and McCall Smith, op. cit., Phillips and Dawson, op. cit. and S. McClean and G. Mather, *Medicine, Morals and the Law* (Aldershot, 1983), ch. 9, but cf. Kottow, op. cit.

50 See Mason and McCall Smith, op. cit., p. 180. It has also been suggested that a doctor who knew that a patient was continuing to drive after he had been advised that it was unsafe for him to do so would be liable in negligence to pay damages to anyone injured by the patient: see 'Doctors, Drivers and Confidentiality', *BMJ* 1 (1974), 399.

51 T. Beauchamp and J. F. Childress, *Principles of Biomedical Ethics* (New York, 1989), p. 338.

52 'Case Histories', *Journal of the Medical Defence Union* (1991), 31.

53 J. Langton and D. Torby, 'Confidentiality and the Sadistic Sex Offender', *Medicine, Science and the Law* 28 (1988), 195.

54 See chapter 1 above [1989] 1 AU ER 1085 and [1990] 2 WLR 471.

55 529 p 22d 553 118 Cal R 129 (1974).

56 See further T. Prior Wise, 'When the Public Peril Begins', 31 *Stanford LR* 165.

57 5551 p 2d 334 131 Cal R 14 (1976), p. 377.

58 See, e.g., *McIntosh v Milano* 403 A 2D 500 NJ Super Ct (1978), where on similar facts to *Tarasoff* a psychotherapist was found liable in a civil damage suit for wrongful death to the parents of a 20-year-old girl killed by her 15-year-old ex-lover. The court held that the duty to warn was a valid concept.

59 The use of this term is more common in the area of promissory estoppel.

60 Report of the Committee on Data Protection (1978) Cmnd 7361.

61 Francis, op. cit.

62 S. Bloch and P. Chodoff, *Psychiatric Ethics* (Oxford, 1991), p. 319.

63 A. Weiss, *Bioethics: Dilemmas in Modern Medicine* (Aldershot, 1985).

64 M. Green, 'Confidentially Speaking', *Journal of Medical Ethics* 8 (1982), 21.

65 Phillips and Dawson, op. cit.
66 See also D. F. Phelby, 'Changing Practice on Confidentiality – A Cause for Concern', *Journal of Medical Ethics* 8 (1982).
67 Working Party on Confidentiality set up by the Steering Committee on Health Services Information Report.
68 D. Campbell and S. Connor, *On the Record: Surveillance, Computers and Privacy* (London, 1986).
69 Seventh Report of the Data Protection Registrar (London, HMSO, 1991).
70 See T. Richards, 'Confidentiality in Question', *BMJ* 303 (1991) 206.
71 See Weiss, op. cit.
72 Hansard, 9 February 1990, pp. 1152 and 1161.

5 PRACTICAL PROBLEMS IN PRIVILEGE ENACTMENT

1 Australian Law Reform Commission Report No. 38, *Evidence* (1987). Canadian Law Reform Commission, *Evidence before the Court.*
2 Australian Law Reform Commission Report No. 38, op. cit.
3 [1977] *Crim LR* 492.
4 *Ibid*, pp. 492–3.
5 See M. Kottow, 'Medical Confidentiality: An Intransigent and Absolute Obligation', *Journal of Medical Ethics* 12 (1986), 117.
6 (1912) 31 NZLR 481.
7 See further J. H. Wigmore, *A Treatise on the Anglo-American System of Evidence*, 3rd edn, Vol. 8 (Toronto, 1983).
8 La 992 173 NW 16 (1870).
9 20 Mich 34, 41 (1871).
10 70 Mo 446 (1882).
11 (1986) 82 Cr App Rep 295 CA.
12 S. 9, 11 Schedule 1 Police and Criminal Evidence Act 1984.
13 S. 62.
14 S. 63.
15 S. 65.
16 S. 62 (10).
17 See I. Younger and M. Goldsmith, *Principles of Evidence* (London, National Practice Institute, 1987), ch. Vi.
18 II NY Rev Stats pt III ch. 7 (1825).
19 For further discussion see 'Developments in Privileged Communications', 98 *Harv LR* 1450, p. 1532.
20 NY CLS CPLR S 4504 (1991).
21 Mental Health Act 1983, ss 2, 3 and 4.
22 For further discussion on the issue of fitness to plead see C. Emmins, *A Practical Guide to Criminal Procedure* (London, 1992, para. 7. 7).
23 S. 28 Evidence Act 1958.
24 See further J. Beigler, 'Psychiatric Confidentiality in the United States Legal System', in ch. 13 of S. Bloch and P. Chodoff, *Psychiatric Ethics* (Oxford, 1984).
25 2 Cal. 3d 415 (1970).

26 See Wigmore, op. cit.
27 See, e.g., Tennessee Code An S 24-1-207, Ohio Revised Code An S 2317.02, Wis Stat S 905.04 (1989-90).
28 See the discussion of Lord Moran's case in J. K. Mason and R. A. McCall Smith, *Law and Medical Ethics* (London, 1987), p. 139.
29 See further J. C. Smith and B. Hogan, *Criminal Law*, 6th edn (London, 1988), p. 319.
30 See M. R. Brazier, *Street on Torts*, 8th edn (London, 1988), pp. 488 onwards.
31 See further Mellows, *Law of Succession*, 4th edn (London, 1983).
32 24 NW 146 (1932).
33 200 Cal 391, 34, 863 (1893).
34 46 Hun 458 12 NYSR 175 (1887).
35 257 NC 32, 38 125 SE 2d 326 (1962).
36 NY CPLR S 4504 (1991).
37 Wis Stat S 905.04 (1989-90).
38 See further *Gillick v West Norfolk and Wisbech AHA* [1986] AC 150 and see generally the discussion in chapter 4 above.
39 Family Law Reform Act 1969, s. 8.
40 [1986] AC 174.
41 NYK CLPR S 4504 (1991).
42 Mass Gen Law Ann Ch 233 S 20.
43 *The Times* (6 June 1991).
44 *Ibid.*
45 M. R. Brazier, *Medicine, Patients and the Law*, 2nd edn (London, 1992), p. 11
46 IU. Code Civ. Proc. s. 8-802; IU.Rev. Stat. ch. 110 8-802 (1984).
47 For a discussion of the question of ethical codes and professional regulation of psychotherapists see J. Holmes and R. Lindley, *The Value of Psychotherapy* (Oxford, 1989), particularly p. 188 onwards.
48 D. B. Hogan, *The Regulation of Psychotherapists, Volume 2: A Study in the Philosophy and Practice of Professional Regulation* (Cambridge, Mass., 1979), ch. 7.
49 I am grateful to Michael Porknoy of the UKSC for Psychotherapy for drawing my attention to this case.
50 Comment, 'Underprivileged Communications: Extension of the Psycho-therapist-Patient Privilege to the Patients of Psychiatric Social Workers', 61 *Calif LR* 1050.
51 See generally W. Reavely, 'Clinical Psychology in Practice', ch. 2 of S. Canter and D. Canter, *Psychology in Practice* (Chichester, 1982).
52 'A Code of Conduct for Psychologists', *Bulletin of the British Psychological Society* (1985), 38, 41-3.
53 See 98 *Harv LR* 1450, p. 1539.
54 NYK CPLR S 4504 (1991); LA Rev Stat Ann S 13-373 A (1); Minn Stat S 595.02 (4) 97; VT Stat Ann tit S 1612 (a) (b).
55 *Professional Conduct and Fitness to Practise*, clause 27 and see J. Seear and L. Walters, *Law and Ethics in Dentistry*, 3rd edn (Oxford, 1991).
56 See generally on the topic of alternative medicine J. Warren-Salmon, *Alternative Medicine, Popular and Policy Perspectives* (London, 1984) and A. Stanway, *Alternative Medicine* (Harmondsworth, 1986).

57 British Medical Association Working Group Report, *Alternative Therapy* (London, 1986).
58 See Stanway, op. cit.
59 *The Independent* (29 August 1990).
60 NYK CPLR S4504 (1991).
61 The freedom of alternative medical practitioners to practise will be curtailed after the formation of the single market in 1992. In other European countries restrictions already exist upon the practice of such therapies.
62 Lexis, for the non-legal reader, is a computerised legal information-retrieval system.
63 United Kingdom Central Council of Nursing and Midwifery, *Code of Conduct* (London, 1992), clause 9.
64 D. Kloss, 'Medical Demarcation' (1988) *Professional Negligence* 14:2, 33.
65 *Neighbourhood Nursing, A Focus for Care* (London, DHSS, 1986).
66 See A. Bowling and B. Sitwell, *The Nurse in Family Practice* (Harrow, 1988), p. 76 onwards.
67 J. D. Finch, *Aspects of Law Affecting the Para-Medical Professions* (London, 1984).
68 Evidence Amendment Act 1980, s. 32 (1) NZ.
69 Ohio Rev Stats, S 400-235 (2) (1985).
70 Report of the Committee on Administrative Tribunals and Enquiries (1957) Cmnd 218.
71 Generally for discussion on tribunals see R.E. Wraith and P.G. Hutchinson, *Administrative Tribunals* (London, 1973) and H.W.R. Wade, *Administrative Law* (Oxford, 1988), ch. 23.
72 [1989] 1 All ER 1045.
73 E. Campbell, 'Principles of Evidence and Administrative Tribunals', in E. Campbell and L. Waller, *Well and Truly Tried* (Sydney, 1982).
74 Mental Health Act 1983, ss 72 and 73.
75 81 Mich 525, 532, 45 NW 977 (1890).
76 150 Misc 669 270 NYS 10 (1934).

6 MEDICAL PRIVILEGE, COSTS AND APPLICATION

1 [1991] *Crim LR* 122.
2 Revised Uniform Rules of Evidence 1974, s. 505. West Virginia is now the only state in America without a clergy–penitent privilege. See generally the discussion in 'Developments in Privileged Communications', 98 *Harv LR* 1450.
3 See discussion in Notes and Comments, 'Functional Overlap between the Lawyer and Other Professionals, its Implications for the Privileged Communication Doctrine', (1962) *Yale LJ* 1126 p. 1246.
4 See McCormick, *Hornbook on Evidence* (St Paul, Minn., 1984), ch. 5, 'Privilege Common Law and Statutory'.
5 See 'Developments: Privileged Communications', 98 *Harv LR* 1450, p. 1575 and also 'Note, Parent–Child Loyalty and Testimonial Privilege',

100 *Harv LR* 910.
6 See 98 *Harv L Rev* 1450 pp. 1611 and 1951 for discussion of the scope of privilege concerning scientists, academics and researchers; see C. R. Knerr and J. D. Carroll, 'Confidentiality and Criminological Research: The Evolving Body of Law' (1978) 68 *Journal of Criminal Law and Criminology* 311.
7 [1972] 3 All ER 219 and see further P. Bromley, *Family Law*, 8th edn (London, 1992), p. 192.
8 [1975] 2 All ER 929.
9 208 Misc 721 144 NYS 2d 820 (1955).
10 If he is not otherwise excluded by the Act see sections 62; 64A; 64 (1) (b); 64 (1) (c); 140 (2) (d) (e); 141 (1); 142 (2) (c); 144 (2); 145 (2); 146 of the Employment Protection Consolidation Act 1978.
11 S. 55(2).
12 *Marshall v Harland and Woolf* (1972) ICR 200.
13 S. 57.
14 [1988] IRLR 510.
15 *Ibid.*, p. 210.
16 *Spencer v Paragon Wallpapers* [1977] ICR 301.
17 J. Bentham, *Judicial Evidence* (1825), chs III, IV.
18 Law Reform Committee, Sixteenth Report (1967) Cmnd 3472.
19 See, e.g., Civil Evidence Act 1968; Police and Criminal Evidence Act 1984; Criminal Justice Act 1988.
20 D. Galligan, 'The Right to Silence' (1988) *CLP* 68.

INDEX

156